# WHY SHOULD I GO TO ANTWERP

# WHY SHOULD I GO TO ↴
# ANTWERP

THE CITY YOU DEFINITELY
NEED TO VISIT
BEFORE YOU TURN 30

# THIS IS WHY!

Antwerp is modest in size, but big in character and culture, with its historical centre, the hip neighbourhood Het Zuid, and the lively area of Berchem. Whether you're a solo traveller, here with friends, or making new connections along the way, this guidebook is designed to help you navigate the best spots in town.

Visiting this vibrant city doesn't have to break the bank. Explore the different areas, take in the scenery, and soak up the atmosphere. Walk, cycle, and use the trams, rather than taking expensive taxis. Book a nice hostel, join walking tours, and visit the famous sights and museums. And don't forget to have a drink along the Scheldt River, or a picnic in a park to experience the local way of life. Because you don't have to go to the expensive boutiques on Schuttershofstraat to find the treasures that truly enrich your life.

This guidebook has you covered with insights into Antwerp's rich history, colourful street art scene, and unique festivals that bring the city to life. Whether you're an art aficionado, a foodie on the hunt for your next culinary delight, or a nightlife ninja ready to conquer the coolest clubs, Antwerp has something just for you. So, pack your curiosity and most comfortable shoes. Antwerp is waiting for you, and it's going to be an amazing ride. One thing is certain, you will want to come back for more.

# CONTENTS

**DISTRICTS** 8
**PRACTICAL INFO** 12

**FOOD AND DRINKS** 100
**GOING OUT** 122

**WHEN TO TRAVEL** 28
**ANTWERP LIFE** 38

**GREEN ANTWERP** 166
**OUTSIDE OF ANTWERP** 182

**SHOPPING** 136

Index 188
Who made this book? 191-192

# DISTRICTS

Despite its modest size, Antwerp boasts a remarkable number of districts. Below are the areas that this guidebook focuses on. Some points of interest are located just beyond them, but we'll point out the nearest district in those cases.

### Historical Centre (Centrum)

The heart of Antwerp, characterised by its rich history, stunning architecture and vibrant atmosphere. It houses iconic landmarks Onze-Lieve-Vrouwekathedraal (Cathedral of Our Lady), Grote Markt (Grand Market Square), and the medieval castle Het Steen. The narrow, cobbled streets are lined with charming cafés, ancient market squares, boutique shops, and historic buildings. Around the lively Ossenmarkt, you can find the University Quarter, with many student bars, cafés, sandwich shops and restaurants.

### Eilandje (North)

Translating to 'Little Island', Eilandje is a historic port area that has undergone extensive redevelopment in recent years. It now boasts waterfront bars, upscale restaurants, and cultural sites such as MAS (Museum aan de Stroom) and the Red Star Line Museum. The marina and historic docks add to its charm, making it a popular destination.

### Centraal Station & Diamant (East)

The Central Station district and the adjacent Diamant form a vibrant cultural hub. Many restaurants and shops are based here. In the former district, you will find Chinatown and one of the oldest zoos in the world, while in the latter, you'll discover the diamond dealers that represent Antwerp's fame in the global diamond trade.

DISTRICTS

### Borgerhout (East)

Energetic street life and a thriving food scene are characteristics of multicultural Borgerhout. It's home to bustling markets, diverse eateries, and eclectic shops. Despite its urban character, Borgerhout also boasts green spaces such as the Te Boelaerpark, providing residents with recreational opportunities. Borgerhout is where your taste buds can take a trip around the world without ever leaving the city.

### Zurenborg (East)

This district is famous for its stunning Belle Époque architecture, characterised by colourful Art Nouveau and neo-Gothic townhouses. It's a picturesque residential area with tree-lined streets, charming squares, and cosy cafés. The street of Cogels-Osylei is particularly renowned for its architectural beauty, attracting visitors eager to admire the decorated façades and refined detailing. This is where the magic of Antwerp truly comes to life.

### Berchem (East/South)

Berchem is a diverse residential area known for its leafy streets, parks, and historic architecture. It offers a peaceful atmosphere away from the hustle and bustle of the city centre. With its tree-lined streets and quaint cafés, it gives friendly neighbourhood vibes. Berchem's lively squares, local markets, and cultural venues contribute to its vibrant community spirit.

### Fashion District & Kaaien (South)

Calling all fashionistas and style mavens, this is your playground! This district is synonymous with Antwerp's thriving fashion industry and home to renowned fashion academies such as the Royal

Academy of Fine Arts. The district is known for designer boutiques and concept stores where haute couture meets high street. The Kaaien, or 'quays', along the Scheldt River are popular for leisurely strolls and outdoor events.

**Het Zuid (South)**

Known as Antwerp's artistic, hip and happening district, Het Zuid is brimming with art galleries, fashionable boutiques, chic cafés, and stylish restaurants. It's a hub for the city's creative community, with its beautiful Belle Époque architecture adding to its allure. The Royal Museum of Fine Arts and the Museum of Contemporary Art are also located here, attracting visitors from all over the world.

**Nieuw Zuid (South)**

This district is a modern extension of Het Zuid, characterised by contemporary architecture, sleek residential blocks, and spacious green areas. It offers a mix of residential, commercial, and recreational spaces, with a focus on sustainable urban development. Nieuw Zuid is rapidly evolving into a vibrant neighbourhood, attracting young professionals and families seeking modern urban living.

**Linkeroever (West)**

Linkeroever, meaning 'Left Bank', is situated on the west bank of the Scheldt River, opposite the city centre. It offers a more tranquil and residential alternative to the bustling city centre, with spacious parks, recreational facilities, and waterfront promenades. Linkeroever provides stunning views of the Antwerp skyline and is popular for outdoor activities such as cycling, jogging, and picnicking.

# TRAVEL

Antwerpen-Centraal is a major hub for domestic and international train services. High-speed trains (Eurostar) connect Antwerp with cities like Brussels, Amsterdam, Paris, and London. Regional and local trains also provide convenient connections to other Belgian destinations. The station itself is a stunning architectural masterpiece worth exploring. Find out more at *belgiantrain.be*.

Several bus companies operate services to and from Antwerp, connecting it with neighbouring cities and countries. The FlixBus network, for example, offers affordable coach services to various European destinations. Visit *flixbus.com* to plan your journey.

If you are travelling by car, keep in mind that traffic congestion can be significant during peak hours (particularly around the Antwerp Ring motorway). Because of the Low Emission Zone (LEZ) and the fact that road parking in the Historical Centre is for permit holders only, it is advisable to park your car at one of the nine P+Rs just outside the city. From there, you can take a tram downtown. Check *slimnaarantwerpen.be* for more info.

Many of Antwerp's attractions, especially those in the Historical Centre, are within walking distance of each other. Exploring the city on foot allows you to soak in the charming architecture, vibrant street life, and hidden gems tucked away in narrow alleyways.

Antwerp is a bike-friendly city. Its dedicated cycling lanes and bike-sharing schemes like Velo Antwerpen, allow both residents

TRAVEL

and visitors to easily rent bicycles for short-term use. Cycling is a popular and eco-friendly way to explore the city, especially given Antwerp's relatively flat terrain and compact city centre. Buy a day (€5) or week (€12) pass online and get the first 30 minutes of each ride for free. Go to *velo-antwerpen.be* to find out how it works.

Bird, Lime, and Poppy offer shared scooters in Antwerp via a free-floating system: they do not have fixed parking spaces, but you locate them with an app. You can unlock a scooter using your smartphone and take off instantly.

Antwerp has an efficient public transport system consisting of trams and buses operated by De Lijn. The city's tram system is particularly convenient for navigating the downtown area and reaching suburban neighbourhoods. A network of buses complements the tram routes, providing connections to areas not served by rail. If you only use the tram or bus once, it's best to opt for a one-time ride (€2.50). If you use public transport more often, a day ticket (€7.50), 10-journey card (€17) or 3-day pass (€15) will work out cheaper. Buy your ticket online and plan your trip via *delijn.be*.

You can take DeWaterbus (a ferry) from Hemiksem or Hoboken towards Steenplein in the city centre. After a stop at Linkeroever, you'll sail straight towards the heart of the port. At any DeWaterbus stop, you can transfer to other forms of transport, or continue by bike. Navigate past traffic jams by boat via *dewaterbus.be*. Cross the Scheldt River between the left and right bank with a free ferry. Bicycles are also allowed free of charge. Check their timetable at *agentschapmdk.be*.

# WHERE TO STAY

**B&B Hotels**

*hotel-bb.com*

This chain has two modern hotels with bright rooms in both Centrum and Het Zuid. Options range from single rooms to family rooms hosting four. Both hotels are wheelchair-accessible with dedicated rooms for disabled guests. There is a vending machine for drinks and snacks, and a breakfast buffet is available at an extra charge.

**A-STAY**

*Pelikaanstraat 86, Centrum, a-stay.com*

Conveniently located next to Antwerpen-Centraal, you will find this urban hotel with 190 rooms. Want to keep up your workout routine? Hit their gym at all hours of the day. No matter the weather, you can always enjoy their urban garden tent to get some fresh air. All rooms have private bathrooms. A-STAY has a 24/7 *grab'n'go* shop and coffee corner. Breakfast is available at an additional charge.

**Antwerp Central Hostel (aka Hostel Pulcinella)**

*Bogaardeplein 1, Centrum, jeugdherbergen.be*

In the heart of the city you will find this hostel with large windows, a bright sleeping area, rooftop terrace, lounge, and bar. They have three room types: for two, four, or six people, each with their own bathroom. Good to know; you will receive a linen package to make your own bed, and towels can be rented. Breakfast is included.

**Antwerp City Hostel**

*Grote Markt 40, Centrum, antwerpcityhostel.be*

Situated in the heart of Centrum, with the Onze-Lieve-Vrouwekathedraal around the corner, you will find this hostel in a Baroque guild house. It even has a façade dating back to 1644. You'll find a shared kitchen, bar, and lounge with a pool table, lockers, luggage storage, and vending machines. There are private and shared (mixed/female) rooms for five to twenty people. Breakfast is included.

**The Ash Hotel**

*Italiëlei 237, Centrum, ash-antwerp.com*

Choose between a shared dorm if you are visiting with a group of friends or a private room when you would like some peace and quiet. They offer female-only dorms as well as mixed dormitories from 3 to 18 guests. With a fully equipped kitchen, a quiet library, and a communal area. Breakfast is not included, but a small morning meal is available at Bar Alma.

**Citybox**

*Molenbergstraat 2, Centrum, cityboxhotels.com*

This affordable design hotel with a Scandinavian touch has accommodation ranging from single occupancy to family rooms, each equipped with its own bathroom. Some rooms come with a balcony. Breakfast can be purchased at the adjacent partner café. In summer, their backyard transforms into a terrace.

**Prizeotel**

*Tunnelplaats 5, Centrum, prizeotel.com*

The area Eilandje is around the corner from this vibrant and colourful hotel with 144 allergy-free rooms with soundproofed windows. The hotel is wheelchair-accessible and has rooms for disabled guests. A breakfast buffet is available at an extra charge.

**Yays**

*Frankrijklei 33, Centrum, yays.com*

Stylish, spacious and fully equipped studios/apartments close to Antwerpen-Centraal. Options range from studios for two people (36 m$^2$) to apartments for six (87 m$^2$). Also suitable for longer stays. No breakfast available.

↓ YUST

**Yust**

*Coveliersstraat 6, East/South, yust.com*

This creative, colourful, and modern hotel is the perfect place to combine staying the night, enjoying some good food, and sipping a few drinks on their rooftop bar. Yust is also known for its workshops, art exhibitions, talks and gigs, where connecting with strangers is at the heart. There are eight-person (mixed and female-only) dorms with shared bathrooms, and two- or four-person rooms with private bathrooms. Also suitable for longer stays. Breakfast is available at an additional charge.

**City Camping at Linkeroever**

*Jachthavenweg 6, West, citycampingantwerp.be*

Are you feeling a bit more adventurous, and would you like to combine the outdoors with the city of Antwerp? Then camping across the Scheldt River is for you. During the summer season (April to November), the camping is open daily, but during the winter season (November to the end of March) only on Saturdays and Sundays. Bring your own tent or rent a tipi or caravan. On Fridays, a food truck comes around, and a small bakery shop is there on weekends.

PRACTICAL INFO

# GOOD TO KNOW

### Language

The primary language spoken in Antwerp is Dutch, but many residents also speak English and French. However, it is appreciated when you attempt basic phrases like: *Goedemorgen* (Good morning), *Goedemiddag* (Good afternoon), *Goedenavond* (Good evening) and *Dank u* (Thank you). The official language may be Dutch, but the spoken language is mainly Antwerps or *Vlaams* (Flemish), which is a dialect/variation of Dutch with its own words.

### Opening Hours

Shops are usually open between 10am and 6pm. Supermarkets are generally open between 8am and 8pm. Many shops and businesses, especially smaller ones, have limited opening hours on Sundays and public holidays. Every first Sunday of the month, and every Sunday in December all shops are open. The antique shops in Kloosterstraat are open every Sunday. Throughout the city, there are many night shops to get the essentials outside of regular opening hours. Check the opening hours of attractions, restaurants, and shops in advance to avoid disappointment.

### Cash

It is wise to have some cash on hand for small purchases, as some places, especially markets and smaller shops, do not accept cards. Cash machines can be scarce in some areas, but on *bankautomaten.be* you can find the nearest one.

## Cuisine

Belgian cuisine is known for its high quality. Don't miss the opportunity to indulge in their chocolate, waffles, Flemish stew, mussels, fries, and beer when you visit. Additionally, Antwerp boasts a diverse culinary scene, with a wide range of international cuisines available in restaurants throughout the city.

## Tipping

Tipping is not obligatory in Belgium. However, it is common to round up the bill or leave a small tip for good service, typically around 5 to 10 per cent.

## Queer

Antwerp is one of the most open-minded and inclusive cities when it comes to acceptance of the LGBTQIA+ community. There are numerous gay bars and clubs dotted throughout the city. The annual Antwerp Pride in August attracts 100,000 participants from dozens of countries.

## Antwerp City Pass

This pass gives you access to lots of tourist attractions, you can use it to travel on public transport, and enjoy lots of discounts. You can buy a pass for 24, 48, or 72 hours. Load the Antwerp City Pass on your smartphone and scan the QR Code in participating museums and attractions. You can buy your pass online at *antwerpcitypass.be*, in person at one of the two Visitor Centres, or at the FOMU museum shop.

## Reduced rates at museums

People up to 25 can visit Antwerp museums at reduced rates, so don't forget to bring Photo ID.

↓ STADSFEESTZAAL

# ANTWERP IN SPRING

In spring, Antwerp locals try to catch every available ray of sunshine. Even when it's still chilly, you'll find them enjoying a cup of coffee outdoors while catching up with friends, wearing some added layers of warm coats and big scarves. It is also the time when locals start to exercise outdoors to enjoy the milder weather. You will see many runners in streets and parks to practise for the Antwerp 10 Miles. This is the largest recreational running event in Belgium and has been held every April since 1986. Is a medal the best souvenir you can possibly imagine? Then sign up and bring your running shoes!

Antwerp's parks and gardens are full of blooming flowers, bursting with tulips, daffodils, and cherry blossoms. The botanical garden Den Botaniek and Stadspark ('City Park') are particularly beautiful in spring. The menus in restaurants change to lighter meals, and seasonal vegetables — like white asparagus — are widely available. Try the 'white gold', as they are often called, Flemish style with hard-boiled egg, parsley and melted butter.

Pentecost, or Whitsun, marks the start of the five-week Sinksenfoor. It is a large fair with over 150 attractions to shake off the winter blues. Don't forget to try some *smoutebollen*; these deep-fried dough balls are a traditional part of every Belgian fair.

# ANTWERP IN SUMMER

Summer in Antwerp is characterised by a lively atmosphere, with buzzing outdoor terraces, and parks filled with people who enjoy picnics, sports or chats. Warm weather also invites swimming at the beach of Sint-Anneke or the natural swimming pond of Boekenberg. You can enjoy summer to its fullest without leaving the city.

Almost every weekend, there is an outdoor (music) festival, event or market to choose from, making the city's energy very vibrant and full of life. During the world-famous Tomorrowland dance festival, you will see people from all over the world carrying the flags of their home countries, creating a cheerful ambience in the streets of Antwerp.

Diversity and love are celebrated annually during Antwerp Pride in August. For several days, thousands of people visit the city to attend events, party together, and to enjoy the highlight: the parade with over 100,000 participants.

Evenings are long and warm and often include an ice cream late at night. The best way to end a hot summer day is by taking a stroll along the Scheldt River to watch the sunset. While Antwerp may not have its own coastline, several urban beach bars appear along the river every year. There you can enjoy a laid-back atmosphere, with sand, sun loungers, cocktails, and if you're lucky, live music.

# ANTWERP IN AUTUMN

With the summer holidays wrapped up, September sees the start of a new academic year. For some reason, it feels like a new beginning each time. Days are shortening, leaves are changing colours, and the cosy season kicks in.

On Saturdays, the (farmers) markets are famous for bringing the freshest produce. This is the season for tasty mushrooms, all kinds of cabbages, pumpkins, and Brussels sprouts, to name a few. If the weather permits, dozens of people sit amidst the market stalls, chatting with friends while enjoying *garnaalkroketten* (shrimp croquettes) and a glass of wine.

Sundays start with freshly baked bread and pastries – make sure to try one of the local *koffiekoeken* – and a good cup of coffee, followed by a visit to a museum, art gallery, or a stroll in one of the parks in or around the city.

Pamper your taste buds at the culinary festival Smaakmeesters in October. More than a hundred restaurants, cocktail bars, and chocolate and other specialty shops offer their signature dishes or delicacies at reduced prices. Embark on a culinary adventure through Antwerp's diverse food scene along different routes, discovering delicious food as you go.

# ANTWERP IN WINTER

Winter brings a festive charm with the city adorned in twinkling lights and decorations. Christmas markets are abundant with seasonal treats, think mulled wine and steaming hot Belgian waffles. Outdoor terraces are heated, so everyone can still enjoy being outside. The cold evenings see restaurants pleasantly filling up, with tables lit by flickering candles. Tickle your taste buds with the Belgian classic *stoofvlees met frieten* (stew with fries). Top it off with a Belgian beer and some cheese, and no rain shower or storm will bother you.

Get a bird's-eye view of the festive lights by hopping on the Ferris wheel. If you'd rather stay grounded, glide to the rhythm of Christmas classics on the ice-skating rink in the heart of the city. Escape the chilly weather by immersing yourself in the warmth of Antwerp's diverse museums. Whether you're a history buff, an art enthusiast, or simply seeking inspiration, there is a museum for every taste and interest.

The first Monday after Epiphany is called Verloren Maandag, 'Lost Monday'. On this day, traditionally, *worstenbroden* (sausage rolls) and *appelbollen* (apple dumplings) are eaten in the city. You will find these treats at many bakeries. And when winter comes to an end, there is always *Pateekesweek*, a week all about pastries and chocolate — the best time to enjoy these Belgian classics!

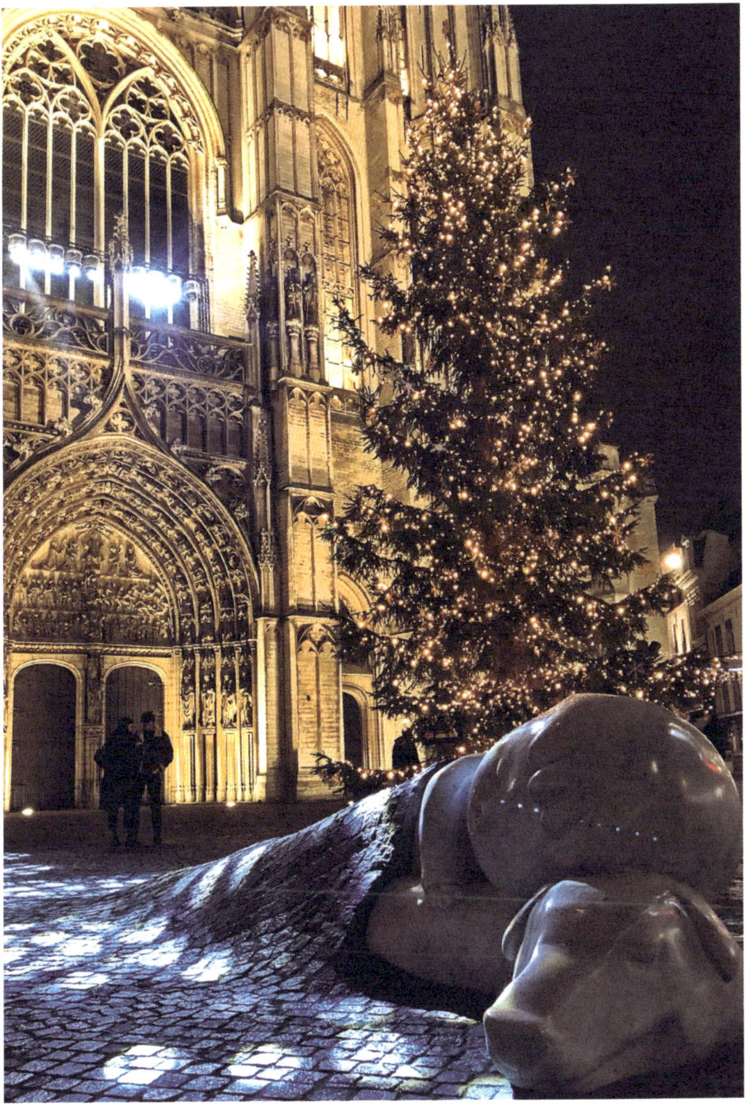

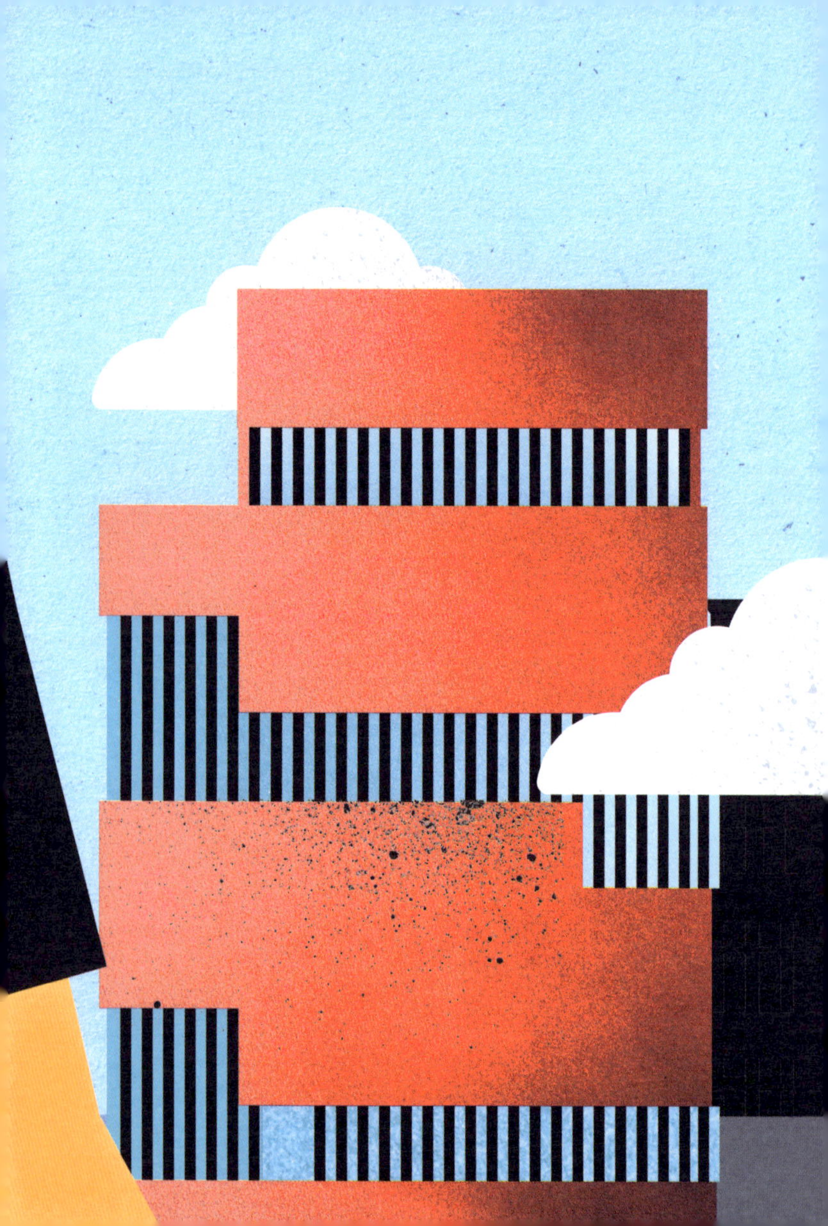

# ANTWERP LIFE

# HISTORY

### Ando-verpus

The Antwerp story starts with the discovery of flint stone utensils from around 35,000 BCE which mark the earliest traces of human presence in Antwerp. The inhabitants, settled near the Scheldt River, lived from agriculture and fishing. Thousands of years later, in 57 BCE, Julius Caesar arrived with his troops in Gallia Belgica. Around 250 CE, the Gallic population comes under the influence of the Romans. Their settlement becomes known as Ando-verpus, and its inhabitants Andouerpi. A Merovingian coin from 726 CE carries the inscription *Anderpus*, which is another early form of the current name Antwerp.

### Early Middle Ages

Fast forward to the Middle Ages, when this underdog transforms into a star player, thanks to its prime spot along the Scheldt. At this strategic river location, the fortress Het Steen is built in the year 1200, making it the oldest standing building of Antwerp today. The Hanseatic League (a powerful network of merchant guilds) comes to town, making Antwerp the cool kid on the medieval trading block. This is also the period when the construction of Antwerp's pride, the Onze-Lieve-Vrouwekathedraal (Cathedral of Our Lady), starts, mid 14th century. It takes 169 years to complete the largest Gothic church of the Low Countries.

## The 16th Century

Now, cue the trumpets for the Renaissance! The arrival of foreign traders introduces exotic goods from distant lands, contributing to the city's reputation as a cosmopolitan centre. The city flourishes, and prosperity and cultural growth significantly increase. In the 16th century, under the rule of the Habsburgs, Antwerp reaches its peak as a commercial and cultural powerhouse. It becomes a haven for artists, intellectuals, and merchants from across Europe. Master painters like Rubens, Jordaens, and Teniers take the stage. The city's port thrives, handling a significant portion of Europe's trade. In 1531, the Bourse, one of the world's first stock exchanges, is founded in Antwerp, reflecting the city's financial relevance. And a few decades later, in 1561, the City Hall is built, which is the mayor's workplace to this day.

## Spanish Influence

During the Spanish occupation of Antwerp in the 16th century, a series of defensive fortifications are constructed. These Spanish ramparts and the infamous 'Spanish Fury' leave a profound mark on the city's history. Under the rule of Emperor Charles V of Spain, these ramparts and bastions are designed to protect Antwerp from outside threats, particularly during the Eighty Years' War. The Spanish Fury in 1576 is also known as the sack of Antwerp. Spanish troops unleash a brutal massacre in the city in response to unpaid wages, resulting in the deaths of thousands of inhabitants and widespread destruction.

## Art & Fashion

When peace returns, the residents of Antwerp gradually become art lovers (and later fashionistas). The Royal Academy of Fine Arts opens

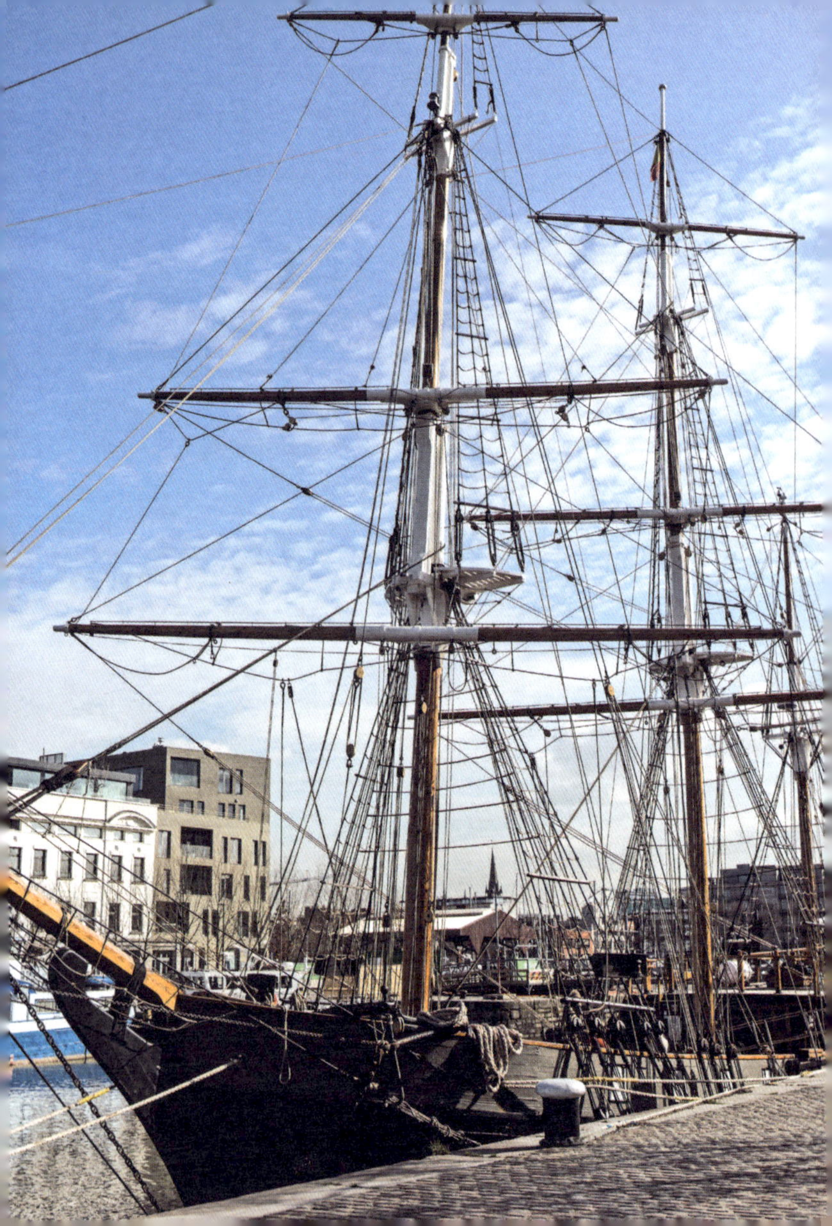

its doors in 1663 as one of the oldest of its kind in Europe. This is the starting point of a revolution in cultural development. Fast-forward 300 years, in the 1960s, the Royal Academy is expanded with the Antwerp Fashion Academy. After about twenty years it comes to full fruition when it produces the famous Antwerp Six. These six Antwerp fashion designers leave a big mark on the fashion scene making it a style capital where creativity knows no bounds. It comes as no surprise that the people of Antwerp are quite fashion forward!

**Napoleon and the Port**

Back to the 18th century. The Industrial Revolution rolls into town, great economic development comes, and Antwerp gets a makeover. Picture cobblestone streets turning into bustling boulevards, and the city growing taller as well as shinier. The construction of a new port connected to the North Sea revives trade. Around 1792, the French army invades Antwerp and seizes the city. Napoleon Bonaparte visits Antwerp in 1803 and modernises the port's infrastructure. The first docks are dug, and shipyards are built. His great ambitions led to expansion, laying the foundation for the second-largest port in Europe.

**Belgian Revolution**

Between 1813 and 1815, what are now the Netherlands, Belgium, and Luxembourg break away from the French empire led by Napoleon. Together, the Netherlands and Belgium form the United Kingdom of the Netherlands, ruled by King William I. But in 1830, crops fail, and supplies decline. And when a revolution breaks out in Paris in July 1830, the unrest spreads to Belgium. This is the starting point of the Belgian Revolution, an armed uprising against King Willem I. It leads to the separation of the southern provinces and the independence of Belgium. This results in the founding of a constitutional monarchy, with Leopold I ascending as the first King of the Belgians. Antwerp remains temporarily occupied, but a little over two years later the city becomes officially part of Belgium in 1832.

**Zoo**

Something completely new emerges, that did not exist anywhere in Belgium before: a real Zoo opens its doors in 1843. Ticket prices are high, so it is only accessible to the wealthy bourgeoisie, who now meet each other in an exotic environment. At first, it is a botanical garden with a few horses, goats, and taxidermy animals. But it continues to expand both in size and animal diversity, with the first okapi ever to be seen outside of Africa. To this day, it remains as one of the oldest zoos in the world.

**World Wars**

The 20th century brings both world wars to Antwerp's doorstep. During World War I (1914-1918), the city suffers German occupation and significant damage during the Siege of Antwerp in 1914. In World War II (1939-1945), Antwerp faces further hardship under Nazi occupation, with the city serving as a strategic target for Allied forces during the Battle of the Scheldt, eventually leading to its liberation in 1944. The post-war period sees efforts to rebuild and modernise, with a focus on preserving the city's historical heritage.

HISTORY

## Summer Olympics

Between these two wars comes some relief: in 1920 the Summer Olympics come to Antwerp. 29 Countries and 2,679 athletes participate, and a total of 25 sports are on the programme. It is the last year that rope pulling was considered an Olympic sport. But it also has some firsts, with the Olympic flag being hoisted for the first time in Olympic history, and the release of doves as a symbol of peace. The age range of the participants is surprising, as the youngest medallist is 14 years old, and the oldest 72.

## World Expo

Ten years later, Antwerp hosts the 1930 World Expo. It is the city's third time, as the expo was held here in both 1885 and 1894. But things are different now, as it is not reserved for just the elite, as better-paid workers can now also afford a ticket. The expo focusses on seafaring, the colonies, and Flemish art, attracting more than 5 million visitors.

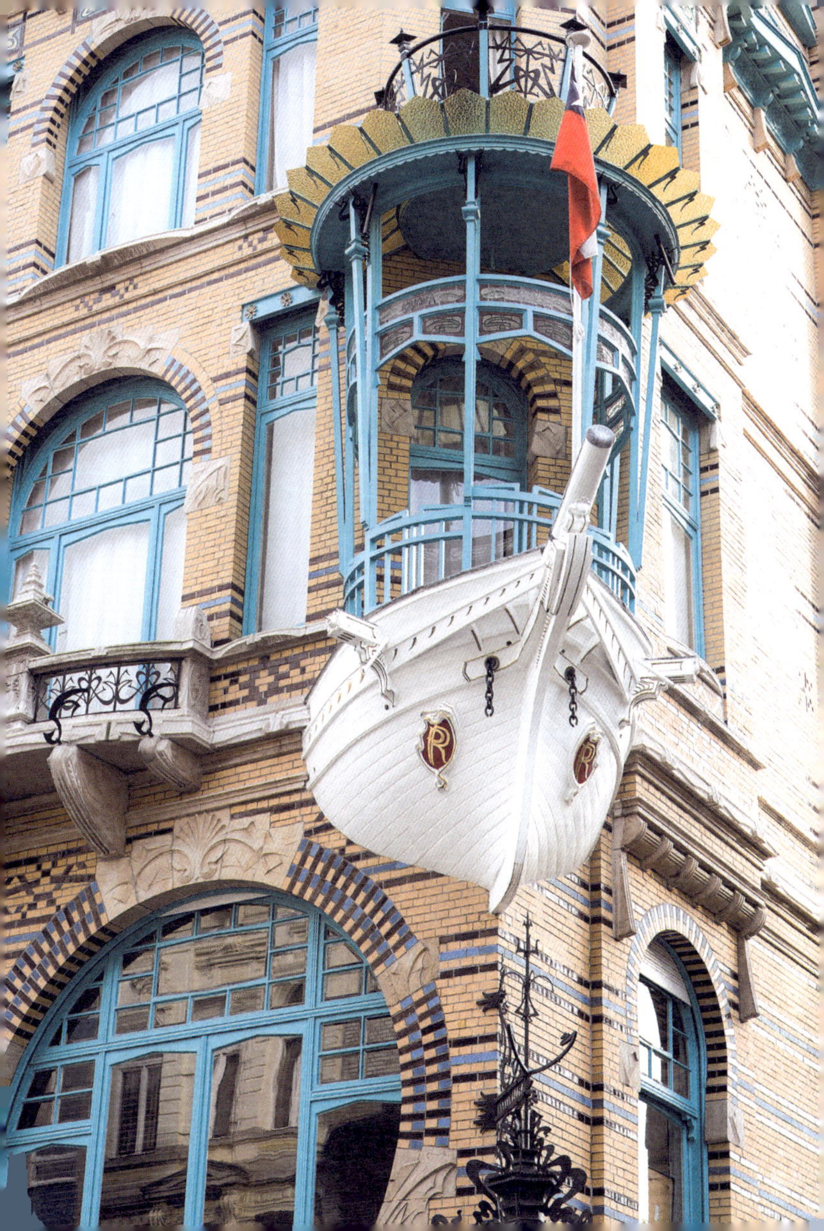

# SIGHTSEEING

**Antwerpen-Centraal**

*Koningin Astridplein 27, Centrum*

Widely regarded as one of the most beautiful railway stations in the world, Antwerp Central Station (dating back to 1905) is a masterpiece blending various architectural styles, including Art Nouveau and neo-Baroque. Its grand dome, decorated façade, and stunning interior with large stairs graced with marble, make it a beloved symbol of the city's transportation hub and a popular attraction.

**Bourlaschouwburg**

*Komedieplaats 18, Centrum, toneelhuis.be*

Stop by the neoclassical Bourlaschouwburg (Bourla Theatre) from 1834 with its elegant façade, adorned with columns and sculptures. Even if you don't visit a performance, you can still enjoy the beautiful interior in their café from Tuesdays to Saturdays. Or savour a brunch at the stunning restaurant on the first Sunday of the month.

**Brabofontein**

*Grote Markt, Centrum*

Depicting the legendary tale of handwerpen (hand throwing), the 1887 Brabofontein (Fountain of Brabo) pays homage to a captivating myth. The story goes that the terrifying giant Antigoon lived in castle Het Steen, demanding toll from every skipper who sailed the river. When someone did not pay, the giant would cut off their right hand and throw it into the river. But one day, a brave Roman called Brabo appeared, defeating the giant, cutting off his hand and throwing it into the Scheldt. Antwerp is said to owe his name to this 'handwerpen'.

**Grote Markt**

*Grote Markt, Centrum*

Nestled within Antwerp's historic heart, you'll find Grote Markt. The market square is lined with beautiful guild houses built by powerful citizens, mostly merchants and craftsmen. The respective patron saints of each trade can be spotted on the roofs of these houses. For example, at number 7, which is known as Pand van Spanje (Spain's building), you can see Saint George just about to impale the dragon. Admire the striking beauty of the UNESCO-listed Renaissance style City Hall (1564) and the Brabofontein, while soaking in the bustling energy of this lively square with its many terraces.

↓ VLAEYKENSGANG

↓ ONZE-LIEVE-VROUWEKATHEDRAAL

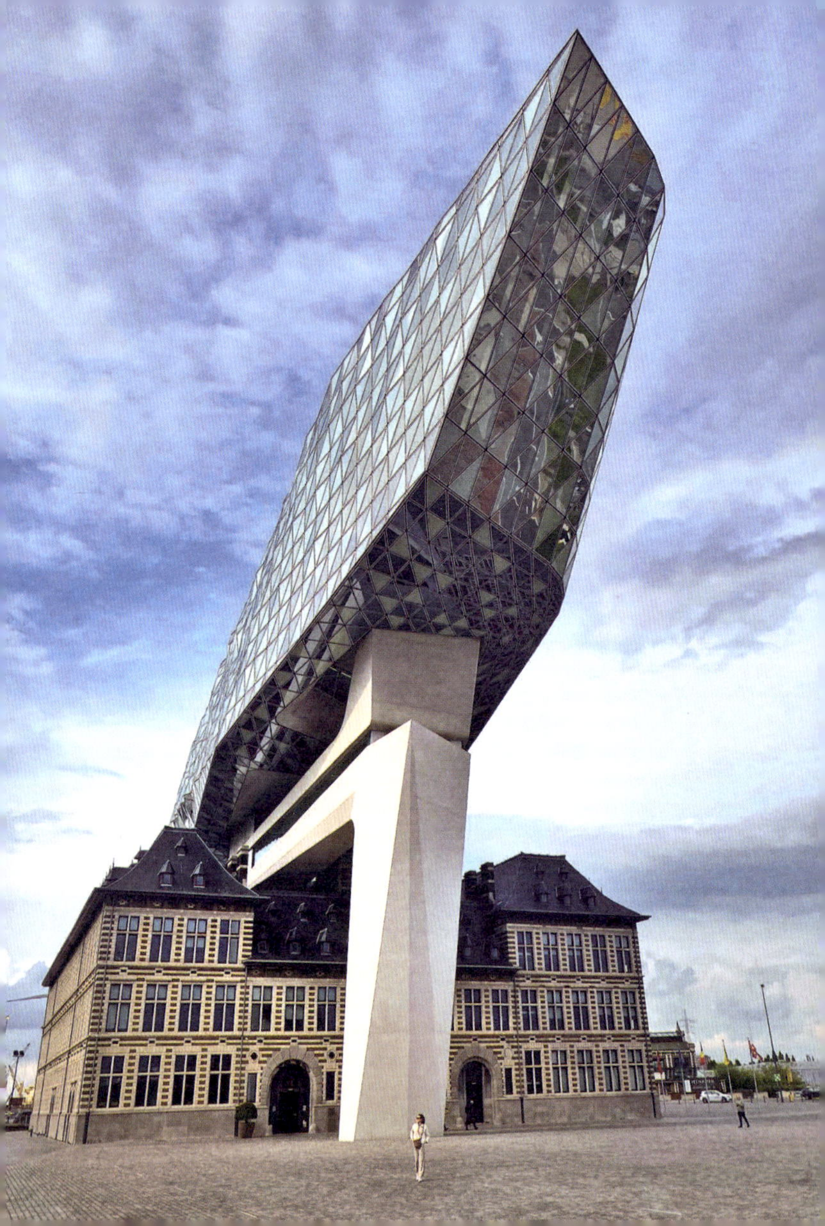

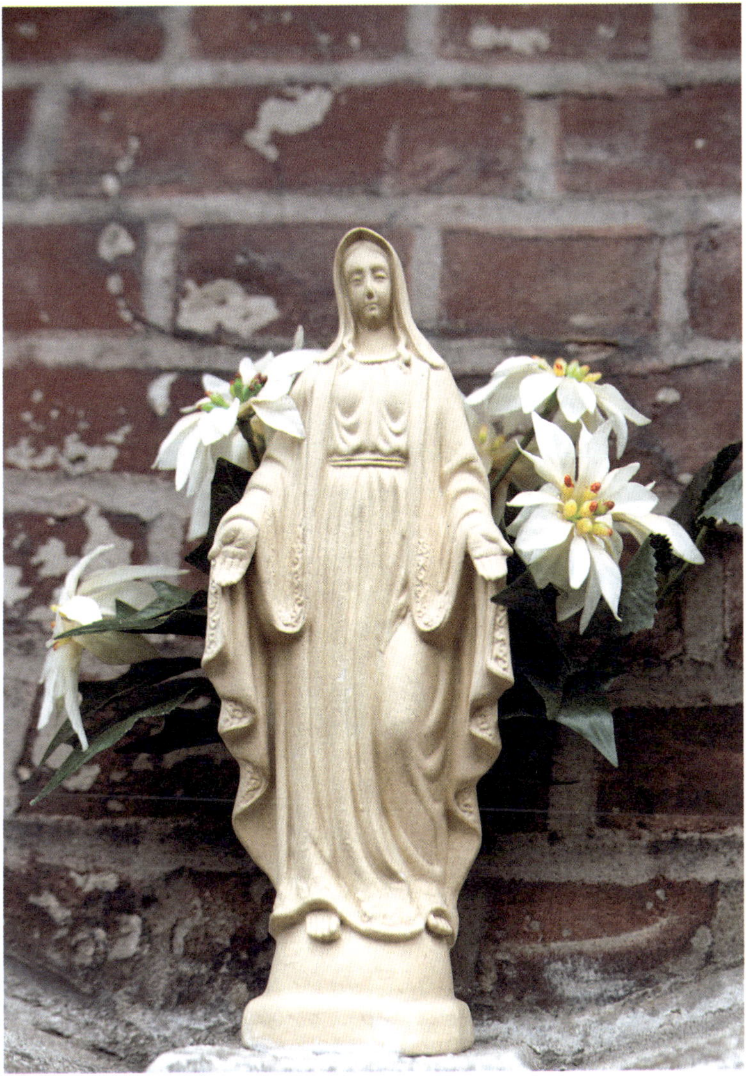

**Oldest house of Antwerp**

*Stoelstraat 11, Centrum*

In the narrow Stoelstraat stands the oldest house of Antwerp. The building dates back to 1546 and has a wooden façade. Also pay attention to the neighbouring houses, as there are some true gems.

**Onze-Lieve-Vrouwekathedraal**

*Groenplaats 21, Centrum, dekathedraal.be*

Standing tall since 1521, the Onze-Lieve-Vrouwekathedraal (Cathedral of Our Lady) is a UNESCO World Heritage Site and an iconic symbol of Antwerp. Marvel at its towering spire, detailed Gothic façade, and stunning interior adorned with masterpieces by Rubens and other Flemish artists. With a height of 123 metres, it is the tallest building in the city. The right tower is much smaller than the left: due to construction conditions and a lack of money, in 1475, construction of the right tower was stopped. In July and August, the carillonneurs perform concerts from the cathedral tower.

**Paleis op de Meir**

*Meir 50, Centrum, herita.beGroenplaats 21, Centrum, dekathedraal.be*

Feel like a royal in Antwerp's famous shopping street the Meir and visit the Rococo style Paleis op de Meir (Palace at the Meir). It was built in 1764 on behalf of the wealthy merchant Van Susteren, and later had owners such as Napoleon Bonaparte (who had it renovated but was never actually there himself) and the Belgian royal family. The furniture is still in Napoleon's personal style, with bright and rich pastel colours and both Egyptian and Roman influences. The palace can only be visited for temporary exhibitions, but the two shops and café are open year-round.

**Sint-Carolus Borromeuskerk**

*Hendrik Conscienceplein, Centrum, visit.antwerpen.be*

For more than 400 years, the Baroque style Sint-Carolus Borromeuskerk has been standing tall at the lovely Hendrik Conscience square. The painting above the church's main altar, with its height of more than five metres, immediately catches the eye. Its unique historical pulley system enables paintings to be changed. You can experience this spectacle on Easter Monday, Ash Wednesday, and during the Night of the Churches in August. The Artists' Mass, with live music by both local as well as international musicians, has been held every Sunday and public holiday for over 75 years. Anyone can attend this mass free of charge at 11.30am.

**Stadsfeestzaal**

*Meir 78, Centrum, stadsfeestzaal.com*

The richly decorated Stadsfeestzaal is Antwerp's most extravagant shopping centre. The building was constructed in Neoclassical style in 1908 mainly to host art exhibitions, antique and book fairs, as well as parties. It was almost lost after a fire in 2000 but has since been rebuilt with many shops and cafés.

**Vlaeykensgang**

*Oude Koornmarkt 16 / Pelgrimstraat 4, Centrum*

This hidden gem, dating back to 1591, is tucked away in the heart of the city. The city's poorest once lived here, together with the shoemakers who, in case of an emergency, had to sound the alarm bell of the nearby cathedral. In the 1960s, the Vlaeykensgang was listed for demolition when it was bought by antiques dealer Axel Vervoordt, who took care of its restoration.

Wander through the narrow cobblestone streets lined with historic buildings and charming restaurants.

**Havenhuis**

*Zaha Hadidplein 1, North, portofantwerpbruges.com*

Havenhuis is a striking architectural marvel that seamlessly blends old and new. Admire the fusion of a historic fire station with a futuristic glass structure (built by world-famous architect Zaha Hadid), symbolizing Antwerp's evolution from bustling port city to modern metropolis. Visits are only permitted on a guided tour.

**Cogels-Osylei**

*Cogels-Osylei, East*

As you wander through Antwerp's charming streets, don't forget to stop by the beautiful neighbourhood of Zurenborg, known for its eclectic mix of Art Nouveau architecture. You will find the most unique buildings in the Cogels-Osylei and the surrounding streets.

**Het Bootje**

*Plaatsnijdersstraat 1, South*

One of the most famous Art Nouveau buildings of the city is called De Vijf Werelddelen (the five continents) and is widely known as 'Het Bootje' (The Little Boat). It was commissioned by a shipbuilder and designed in 1901 with a boat-shaped balcony. It is located behind the Royal Museum of Fine Arts. Stroll past it during a walk through the museum park.

↓ VOETGANGERSTUNNEL

**Voetgangerstunnel**

*Kaaien / West*

Cross the 572-meter long Voetgangerstunnel (pedestrian tunnel) or Sint-Annatunnel with its antique escalators to Linkeroever, for the best skyline view of Antwerp from the left bank. You can enter the tunnel from the city side via Sint-Jansvliet, and from Linkeroever via Frederik van Eedenplein.

# MUSEUMS

**The Antwerp Story**

*Steenplein 1, Centrum,*
*visit.antwerpen.be*

Embark on a journey through the city's rich history, culture, and heritage via the immersive experience that is The Antwerp Story. Follow the trail through eleven rooms and get to know the city's neighbourhoods, marvel at scale models of architectural masterpieces, and listen to the stories of its diverse inhabitants. End your tour on the roof terrace from where you will have beautiful views of the city.

**Chocolate Nation**

*Koningin Astridplein 7,*
*Centrum,*
*chocolatenation.be*

Dive into the history and culture of Belgian chocolate at Chocolate Nation. This interactive museum offers visitors a sensory experience, showcasing the journey of cocoa from bean to bar through multimedia displays, tastings, and demonstrations. Chocolate Nation celebrates Belgium's reputation as a world-renowned chocolate producer and explores the country's deep-rooted love affair with this sweet delicacy. Warning: visiting may cause extreme cravings!

**DIVA**

*Suikerrui 17-19, Centrum,*
*divaantwerp.be*

Antwerp's rich tradition of shiny craftsmanship and sparkling luxury goods is celebrated at DIVA. Located in Centrum, the museum offers visitors a fascinating journey through the world of diamonds, showcasing precious gemstones, exquisite jewellery, and luxurious silverware. DIVA explores the history, artistry, and cultural significance of these items, highlighting Antwerp's role as a global hub for the diamond trade.

**MoMu**

*Nationalestraat 28, Centrum, momu.be*

This is not your average fashion pit stop – it's a runway of imagination, or a catwalk of creativity. The MoMu (ModeMuseum; Fashion Museum) is dedicated to showcasing the rich history and evolution of fashion. It features exhibitions that explore its various aspects, from historical garments to contemporary designs. MoMu aims to celebrate Antwerp's status as fashion capital and its contributions to the global fashion industry. From haute couture to street chic, this museum celebrates the art of dressing to impress.

↓ MUSEUM MAYER VAN DEN BERGH

↓ THE ANTWERP STORY

**Museum Mayer van den Bergh**

*Lange Gasthuisstraat 19, Centrum, museummayervandenbergh.be*

Fritz Mayer van den Bergh was a Belgian art collector who assembled a remarkable collection of medieval and Renaissance artworks during the late 19th century. Housed in a neo-Gothic mansion, the museum showcases his eclectic collection, which includes paintings, sculptures, tapestries, and decorative arts. Highlights include works by Pieter Bruegel the Elder, Hieronymus Bosch, and Hans Memling.

**Museum Plantin-Moretus**

*Vrijdagmarkt 22, Centrum, museumplantinmoretus.be*

Experience French vibes at this UNESCO World Heritage Site which is one of the oldest printing museums in the world. Museum Plantin-Moretus is housed in the former home and workshop of Christophe Plantin, a prominent 16th-century French printer and publisher. The museum showcases a vast collection of printing presses, typefaces, manuscripts, and rare books, offering insights into the history of printing and publishing in Antwerp.

**Rubenshuis**

*Hopland 13, Centrum, rubenshuis.be*

The Rubenshuis is the former residence and studio of the renowned Flemish Baroque painter Peter Paul Rubens. Located in the heart of Antwerp, Rubenshuis is a historic house that preserves the artist's living quarters, art collection, and studio space. While currently undergoing a renovation (with the artist's home reopening in 2027), the museum typically offers visitors a glimpse into Rubens's life and artistic work through its extensive collection of paintings, sketches, and personal belongings. The new visitor centre has opened its doors in the summer of 2024. It houses an immersive experience, library, and a new Baroque garden containing 17,000 plants.

### MAS

*Hanzestedenplaats 1, North, mas.be*

MAS (Museum Aan de Stroom; Museum by the Stream) is a striking architectural landmark along the Antwerp waterfront. The museum focuses on the city's cultural heritage, exploring themes such as maritime history, global trade, and multiculturalism. Its collection includes artifacts, artworks, and interactive displays that offer insights into Antwerp's past, present, and future. Don't forget to soak in the panoramic views of the city from its rooftop terrace (free to visit).

↓ KMSKA

**Red Star Line Museum**

*Montevideostraat 3, North, redstarline.be*

The history of emigration from Europe to North America is uniquely displayed at the Red Star Line Museum, which focuses on the Red Star Line shipping company that operated from Antwerp in the late 19th and early 20th centuries. It tells stories of millions of immigrants who embarked on transatlantic journeys in pursuit of a better life in the New World. The museum celebrates the courage, resilience, and diversity of the human spirit, and the place where dreams set sail and journeys begin. Nice to know: Albert Einstein was a regular guest on the Red Star Line's ocean steamers.

**FOMU Fotomuseum**

*Waalsekaai 47, South, fomu.be*

Photography and visual culture play a central role at photo museum FOMU. Its collection features rotating exhibitions that showcase both historical and contemporary photography, highlighting the work of local and international photographers. Wander through halls covered with images that provoke, inspire, and transport you to far-off lands or inner realms. Get ready to see the world through a new lens.

↓ MAS & MARINA

**KMSKA**

*Leopold de Waelplaats 1, South, kmska.be*

The *grande dame* of all museums in Antwerp for sure is KMSKA, Koninklijk Museum voor Schone Kunsten Antwerpen (Royal Museum of Fine Arts Antwerp). After more than ten years of renovation, this prestigious fine-art museum boasts an extensive collection of artworks, including paintings, sculptures, and drawings, primarily focusing on Flemish and Belgian artists. Some of the highlights include works by renowned masters such as Peter Paul Rubens, Anthony van Dyck, and Jacob Jordaens. The museum garden, with its beautiful statues, is also worth a visit.

**M HKA**

*Leuvenstraat 32, South, muhka.be*

Nestled in the beautiful Het Zuid area you will find M HKA, the leading institution for contemporary art in Antwerp. It houses a diverse collection of modern and contemporary artworks, including paintings, sculptures, installations, and video art. The museum is known for its innovative exhibitions that explore relevant social, political, and cultural issues, as well as its support for emerging artists.

↓ TOP: M HKA / BOTTOM: MOMU

MUSEUMS

# STREET ART

From the city centre to the outskirts of Antwerp; you will find street art by famous as well as lesser-known artists everywhere. The free *Street Art Cities* phone app is a useful tool to spot them all.

**Cartoon Murals**

*stripmuren.be*

Antwerp is dotted with cartoon murals, adding a playful touch to its streets. These murals by Muurvast feature well-known characters (like Suske & Wiske) or original creations by local artists. Follow the *Stripmurenroute* to see them all.

**Charlotte De Cock**

*Pelikaanstraat 86, Centrum*

Next to Antwerpen-Centraal, you'll find one of Charlotte De Cock's murals. She is famous for her monochrome portraits of animals, people (Troonplaats 3-5), and mushrooms (Sint-Jansvliet 21). In this case, expect to see black and white pelicans, referring to the name of the street, and adding a unique touch to a hotel entrance.

**Dzia & SMOK**

*Metrostation Plantin, Centrum*

At a metro station, you'll find artworks by Dzia (a fox) and by SMOK (a fish). Dzia is known for his geometric animal designs, while SMOK's work often features animals in surreal settings. These artworks add visual interest to the station, transforming it into a more dynamic space.

**El Mac**

*Gramayestraat 9, Centrum*

Known for his striking portraits, El Mac often features subjects with a sense of admiration and introspection. His tribute *Mural for my Father* is characterised by El Mac's signature use of bold lines and shading techniques.

**Kopstraatje**

*Kopstraatje, Centrum*

This little alley leading from Kammenstraat to Nationalestraat showcases a variety of street art pieces created by different artists. Expect a diverse range of styles, techniques, and themes as you explore this little passage.

**Pablo Piatti**

*Vrijdagmakt 7, Centrum*

*Memories of a Geisha* features a depiction of a geisha, inspired by Japanese culture and aesthetics, and referring to the Japanese-inspired restaurant in the building. Look for Pablo Piatti's delicate brushwork, complex details with flowers, and vibrant colours, characteristic to his style.

STREET ART

**Super A**

*Haringrodestraat 104, East*

Dutch artist Super A is known for his hyper-realistic style and creative compositions. On Brewery De Koninck's building, he made a piece with enormous colourful pigeons in the foreground, and Antwerp's beloved cathedral in the background.

**Street Art Wall**

*Minckelersstraat, East/South*

The Minckelersstraat in Berchem hosts many street art pieces by various artists over a length of 300 metres. Expect to encounter a mix of styles and subjects, contributing to the eclectic atmosphere of the neighbourhood. Berchem even has its own free street art walking map, which you can get at one of the two Visitor Centres of Visit Antwerp, or at Berchem's district office at Grotesteenweg 150.

**SMOK**

*Walemstraat 63, East/South*

Antwerp born and raised SMOK is recognisable by his playful artworks, often featuring animals. In *Catifiction*, a large cat lays down, looking over a parking lot. With a very cool optical illusion.

**Zentih**

*Brederodestraat 9, South*

Antwerp's famous (Hollywood) actor Matthias Schoenaerts is also a popular graffiti artist who goes by the name of Zenith. The mural *Fissures & Flaws* is his collaboration with Steve Locatelli, another famous Antwerp graffiti artist. The piece represents cracks, scars, and defects that Matthias has seen and photographed around the world. Another of his beautiful murals is *Humain*. Zenith depicted a hand on a

50-meter-high façade. It has multiple meanings, and as it represents connection, it also refers to Belgian's colonial past. You can find it on Kronenburgstraat 45 (Het Zuid).

↓ HUMAIN BY ZENITH

STREET ART

# CINEMA

**Cinema Cartoon's**

*Kaasstraat 4-6, Centrum, cinemacartoons.be*

Since 1978, Cinema Cartoon's has been offering a range of films appealing to all ages: from in-depth documentaries, award-winning feature films, modern classics, and small audience films to unconventional genre films.

**De Cinema**

*Maarschalk Gérardstraat 4, Centrum, destudio.com*

De Cinema at De Studio is buzzing with energy and creativity. This multifaceted venue serves as a platform for various artistic endeavours, including theatre productions, live performances, and exhibitions. The eclectic mix of films ranges from documentaries and family films to contemporary indie releases and classic retrospectives.

**Filmhuis Klappei**

*Klappeistraat 2, North, klappei.be*

Filmhuis Klappei is a hidden gem, cherished by cinephiles for its intimate atmosphere and diverse programming. Nestled within a historic building, this cosy cinema offers an eclectic mix of films, including arthouse gems, cult classics, and experimental works.

**De Roma**

*Turnhoutsebaan 286, East, deroma.be*

De Roma is a cultural institution that has been an integral part of Antwerp's entertainment scene for generations. Housed in a magnificent Art Deco building, De Roma boasts grandeur and history. Known for its live performances, it also hosts film screenings, from classic Hollywood epics to contemporary world cinema.

**Cinema Lumière**

*Lakenstraat 14, South, lumiere-antwerpen.be*

Situated within FOMU, Cinema Lumière offers a diverse selection of high-quality films across two screening rooms. The focus lies on contemporary films, but with a consideration for classics and restorations, thematic screenings, and family films.

↓ DE CINEMA

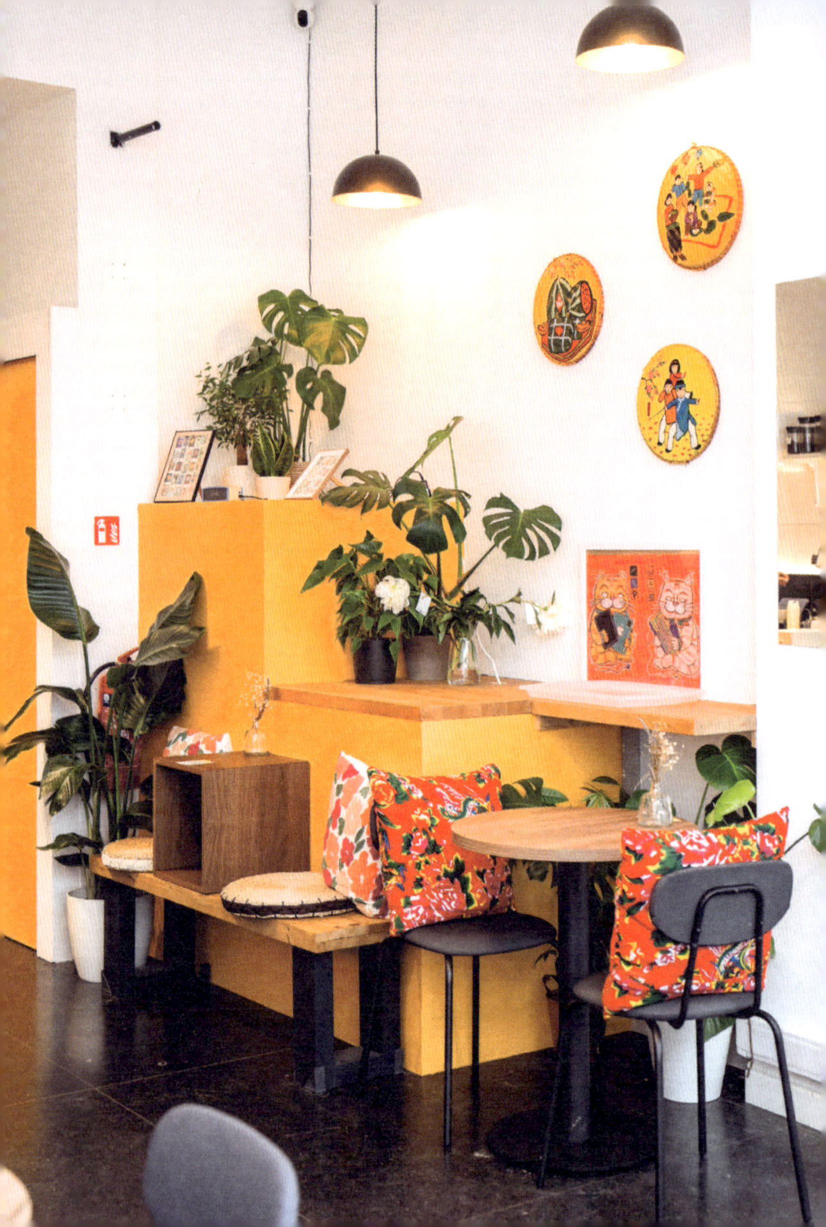

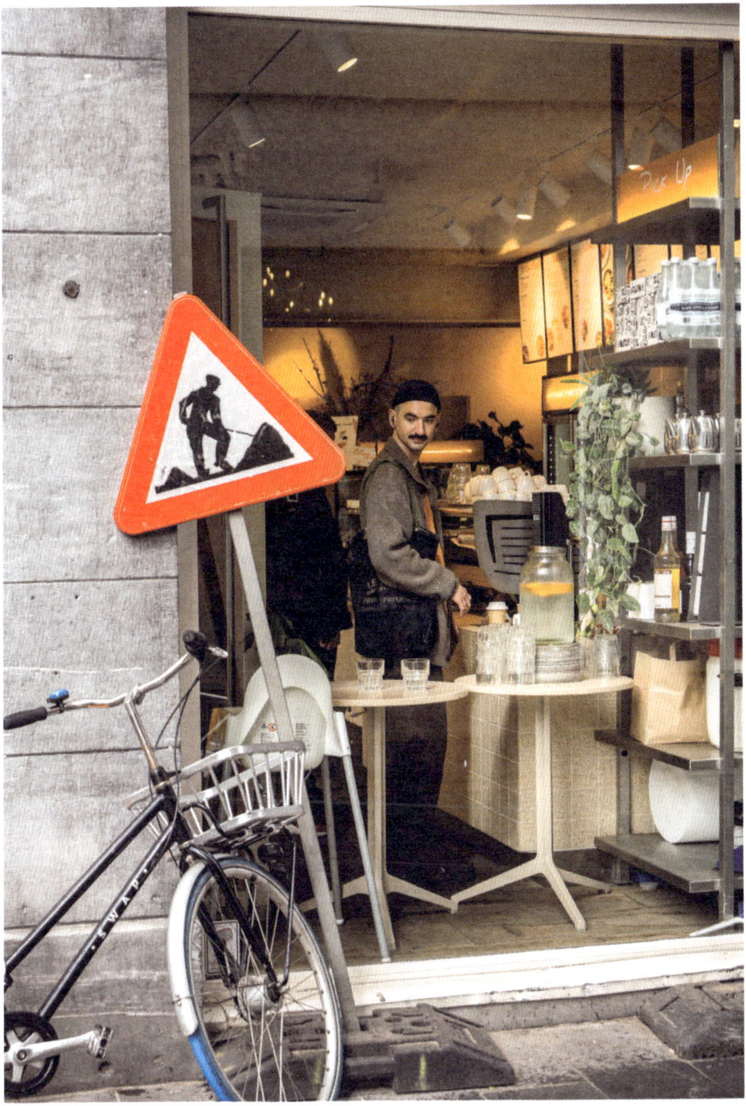
Pick Up
SWAP

# FESTIVALS

### Antwerp Art Weekend

A weekend of art exhibitions, installations and performances across various venues and galleries, showcasing local and international artists.

*antwerpart.be*

### Antwerp Pride

A celebration of diversity, equality, and LGBTQIA+ rights. The LGBTQIA+ community and allies come together to celebrate love with many events throughout the city culminating into the parade.

*antwerppride.com*

### Sinksenfoor

Whitsun (Pentecost) marks the start of the largest fair of Belgium: the five-week Sinksenfoor. *Sinksen* is the Flemish word for Whitsun. The *foor* (fair) brings you not only roller coasters and Belgian waffles but also *smoutebollen*, typical Belgian deep-fried dough balls.

*Spoor Oost, East, insta @sinksenfoor*

### Antwerpen Proeft

A culinary multi-day festival at Waagnatie, where foodies can sample gourmet dishes and enjoy cooking demonstrations as well as workshops by renowned chefs.

*Rijnkaai 150, North, proeft.be*

### Jazz Middelheim

The prestigious jazz festival at Park Den Brandt features world-class jazz musicians and bands, offering performances that range from traditional to avant-garde.

*Beukenlaan, South, jazzmiddelheim.be*

### Tomorrowland

As one of the world's largest electronic music festivals, Tomorrowland attracts a crowd from across the globe for a weekend of extravagant stages, top-tier DJs, and an immersive experience. Outside of the city.

*De Schorre, Boom, tomorrowland.com*

## ZOMER VAN ANTWERPEN
## THE 'SUMMER OF ANTWERP' INCLUDES:

**Live is Live**
Three days of world-class music, *liveislive.be*

**Transit Festival**
One-day showcasing progressive electronic music, *transit-festival.com*

**Borgerrio**
Free family-friendly festival, held every other year, *insta @borgerrio*

**FESHTA**
Family-oriented free festival, *insta @nuffsaidlive*

**Contrair Open Air**
A day of electronic music, *contrair.be*

**Vaag Outdoor**
A haven for techno, rave, and melodic house fans, *clubvaag.be*

**Thorn in My Side Festival**
One-day rock festival, *thorninmysidefestival.be*

# TOURS

### Bike Tour

Experience Antwerp from a different perspective. Led by local guides, you'll pedal through historic streets, bustling neighbourhoods, and scenic parks, while learning about the city's landmarks, culture, and lifestyle.

*antwerpbiketours.eu, antwerpbybike.be*

### Brewery De Koninck

Go on a tour of the city brewery to see the production process and learn everything about the craft of brewing. End your tour with a taste of real Antwerp beer such as a *Bolleke* or Tripel D'Anvers.

*dekoninck.be*

### Harbour Boat Tour

Discover the bustling port of Antwerp from the water on a scenic boat tour through the harbour. Admire impressive ships, cargo terminals, and industrial landscapes while learning about the port's history, operations, and economic significance.

*flandria.nu*

### De Ruien

Explore Antwerp's hidden history by venturing into the underground network of canals and former sewage system known as De Ruien. Led by knowledgeable guides, visitors can delve into the city's past, discovering secrets and stories while navigating these ancient waterways.

*ruien.be*

**Vegan Food Tour**

Embark on a culinary journey through Antwerp's vibrant vegan food scene on this specialised food tour. Participants will explore a variety of plant-based eateries and taste delicious dishes.

*nom-eat.be*

**Walking Tour**

Immerse yourself in Antwerp's rich history and lively culture on a walking tour with a local guide. Explore iconic landmarks, charming neighbourhoods, and hidden gems while learning about the city's fascinating stories and legends.

*experienceantwerp.be/en/city-walks*

# THINGS TO DO

**CHIYU**

The ancient Japanese art of *kintsugi* takes centre stage at CHIYU. This restoration workshop celebrates imperfection and resilience through the art of repairing broken objects with a golden lacquer.
*chiyu-kintsugi.com*

**Graffiti Shop Artifex**

At Graffiti Shop Artifex, aerosol cans transform into tools of expression. Participants learn different techniques under the guidance of skilled graffiti artists.
*graffitishopartifex.be*

**Listen to your Art**

Unleash your inner artist in workshops that offer a supportive environment for artistic exploration. Learn basic techniques of drawing and painting like Basquiat, David Hockney, or Renoir, or join a 'Paint & Sip Party with Bob Ross'.
*Meirbrug 1, Centrum, listentoyourart.be*

**Sukoon Studio**

This workshop offers a serene retreat for pottery enthusiasts of all levels. Participants learn hand-building as well as wheel-throwing techniques.
*Oude Leeuwenrui 34a, Centrum, sukoon.studio*

**De Groene Stadshut**

Delve into the world of natural and sustainable body care products. Craft your own soap, shampoo bars, lip balms, body scrubs, and more.
*Bredestraat 44, Centrum/South, degroenestadshut.be*

## House Raccoon

Explore the art of terrazzo at House Raccoon. Craft exquisite items that blend coloured chips with resin to create striking patterns and textures.
*Montevideostraat 6c, North, houseraccoon.be*

## Studio Fluo

Studio Fluo offers a range of creative experiences, from traditional handicrafts to contemporary DIY projects, such as screen printing, ceramics, glass art, paper crafting, and more.
*Ballaarstraat 32/1, East/South, studio-fluo.be*

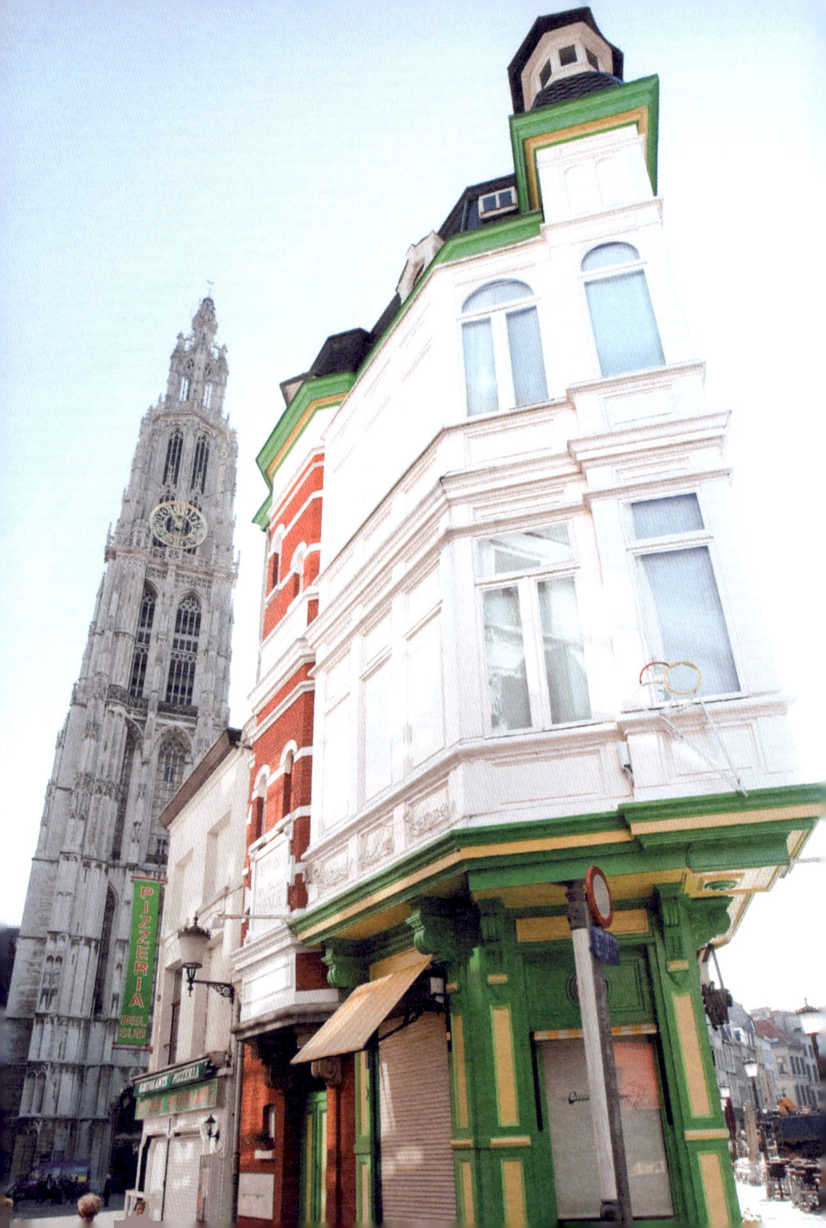
PIZZERIA
DEL SUD

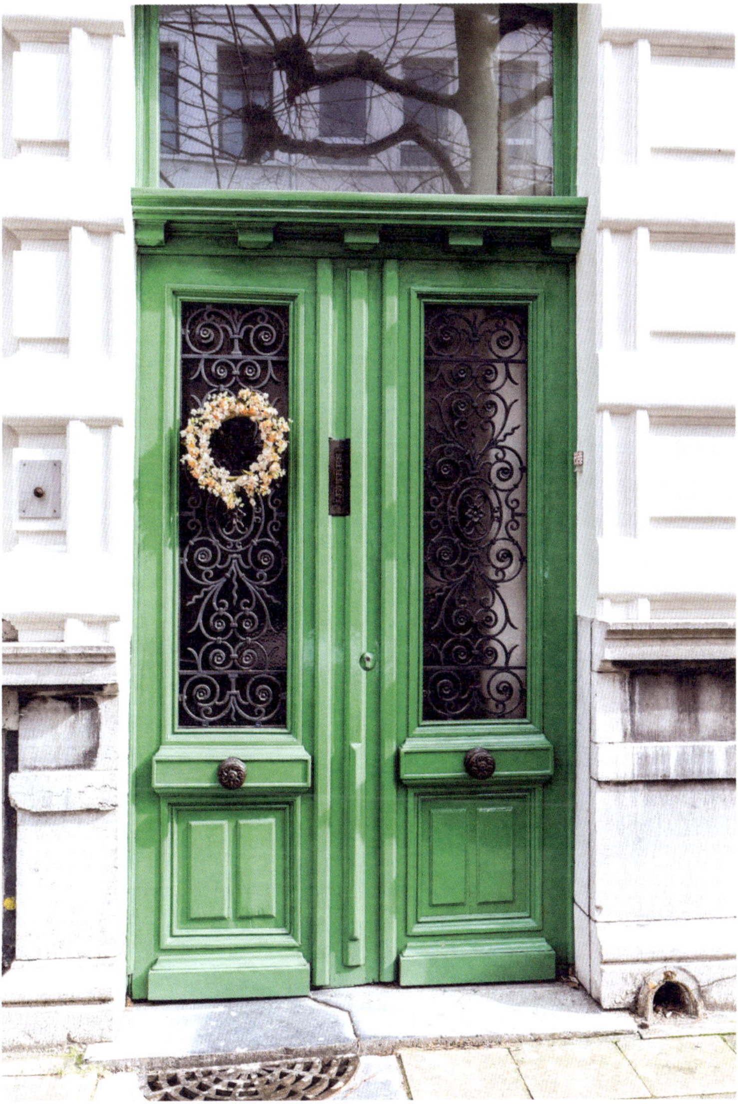

# FAMOUS PEOPLE

### Alex Agnew

Agnew is a beloved figure in Antwerp's comedy scene and one of Belgium's most successful stand-up comedians. He is known for his sharp wit and unapologetic observations on contemporary society. He is also the singer of a hard rock band as well as a co-presenter of the podcast *Welcome to the AA*.

### Toby Alderweireld

Famous for his talent on the football pitch, Alderweireld has made a name for himself on the international stage. Representing both Belgium and prominent European clubs like Ajax, Altético Madrid, Tottenham Hotspur, and Al-Duhail. Since 2022, he has been back in his beloved hometown, playing as a defender for Royal Antwerp.

### Romelu Lukaku

A formidable striker, Lukaku's skills on the football pitch have made him one of Belgium's most admired sporting icons. With his exceptional goal-scoring ability, he has achieved success at the highest levels of the sport. He played at clubs such as Chelsea, Everton, Manchester United, and AS Roma.

### Milow

With melodic compositions and heartfelt lyrics, talented singer-songwriter Milow touches many hearts. The fusion of folk, pop, and indie rock creates his distinctive sound. He earned praise for his most famous songs *You don't know*, *Ayo Technology*, and *You and me*.

**Christophe Plantin**

French-born Christophe Plantin is famous for his significant contributions to the printing and publishing industry during the Renaissance. As the founder of Plantin Press, he played a crucial role in the spreading of knowledge throughout Europe, producing beautifully crafted books that showcased careful attention to detail and artistic excellence. Plantin's legacy continues to resonate in Antwerp, as his former residence is now Museum Plantin-Moretus, a UNESCO World Heritage Site celebrating the art of printing.

**Peter Paul Rubens**

One of Antwerp's most celebrated inhabitants is German Baroque master painter Rubens, whose dynamic brushwork and richly expressive style revolutionised European art. Famed for his mythological scenes, religious works, and impressive portraits, Rubens' influence extended far beyond his hometown, securing Antwerp's reputation as a cultural hub in the 16th century. The Rubenshuis, his former residence and studio, now serves as a museum dedicated to his life and works, offering visitors a glimpse into the artist's creative genius (see page xxx).

**Matthias Schoenaerts**

Actor Matthias Schoenaerts has gained recognition for his captivating performances both at home and abroad. He has acted with big names such as Clive Owen, Mila Kunis, and Margot Robbie to name a few. His CV includes *Loft*, *De Rouille et d'Os*, *A Little Chaos*, *Le Fidèle*, *Django*, *Red Sparrow*, and *The Old Guard*. Another way to unleash his creativity is as graffiti artist Zenith.

**Laura Tesoro**

Known for her powerhouse vocals and dynamic stage presence, Laura Tesoro commands the spotlight with her charisma. She represented Belgium in the Eurovision Song Contest in 2016 with her song *What's the Pressure*. Nowadays, Laura is one of four coaches in *The Voice Kids* in Flanders.

**Dimitri Vegas & Like Mike**

World-renowned DJs and producers Dimitri Vegas & Like Mike may not have been born in Antwerp, but they have helped propel Antwerp's/Belgium's electronic music scene to global fame. With their high-energy sets and infectious beats, these brothers have become a fixture at major festivals and clubs worldwide.

**Tom Waes**

Actor, director and TV presenter Tom Waes is known for daring and adventurous television programmes. For *Reizen Waes*, he visits dangerous and surprising places around the world that the average tourist ignores. He is also known for his role in the Netflix series *Undercover*, as well as a series about ordinary people undergoing tests for the Special Forces, called *Kamp Waes*.

## THE ANTWERP SIX

This group of avant-garde fashion designers rose to international fame in the 1980s, collectively shaping the landscape of contemporary fashion with their innovative designs and rebellious spirit.

**Ann Demeulemeester**

First of the Antwerp Six is Ann Demeulemeester. Her style is characterised by a fusion of dark romanticism, minimalism, and avant-garde aesthetics. She founded her label in 1985, quickly gathering attention for her unconventional designs that challenged traditional beliefs of femininity and masculinity.

**Dries Van Noten**

Dries Van Noten is celebrated for his eclectic and innovative designs that seamlessly blend craftsmanship, prints, and textures. He launched his label in 1986, quickly gaining recognition for his bold use of colour, rich textiles, and complex embellishments.

### Walter Van Beirendonck

Fearless creativity is the force behind Walter Van Beirendonck's strikingly distinct designs, featuring bold colours, graphic prints, and playful motifs. He challenges societal norms, exploring themes of gender, identity, and sexuality. He was artistic director of the fashion department of the Royal Academy of Fine Arts and a lecturer for almost forty years.

### Dirk Bikkembergs

The fusion of sportswear and high fashion was introduced by Dirk Bikkembergs. After launching his (online) label, he gained attention for his innovative approach to menswear. Bikkembergs' designs often feature athletic influences, such as football kits and motorcycle gear, reinterpreted through luxurious fabrics and detailed tailoring.

### Dirk Van Saene

Dirk Van Saene is known for his experimental approach to fashion. His label gained recognition for his innovative use of textiles, unconventional silhouettes, and deconstructive techniques. Van Saene's designs often blur the lines between art and fashion.

### Marina Yee

Last but not least is Marina Yee. She started her career working for Maison Martin Margiela before launching her own label. Marina Yee has since then been known for her conceptual approach to fashion. Her designs often feature draped fabrics and innovative construction techniques. She criticises overconsumption, using recycled materials as much as possible.

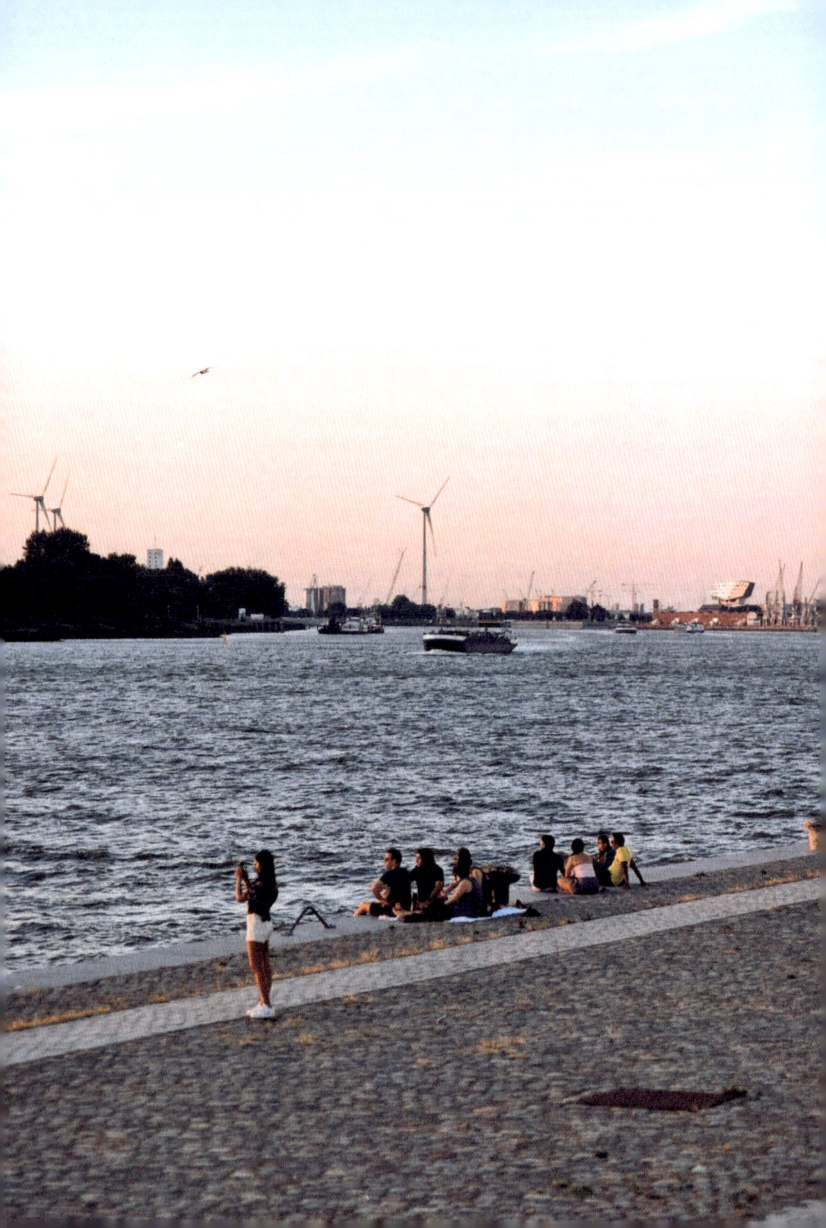

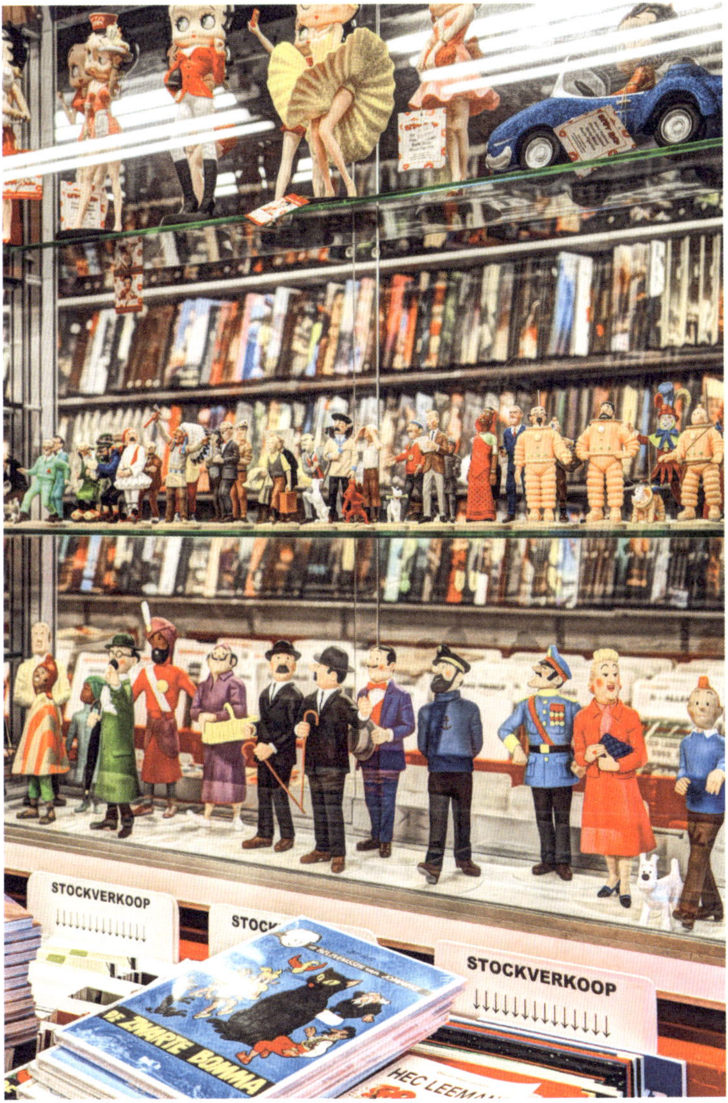
STOCKVERKOOP
STOCKVERKOOP
DE ZWARTE BOMMA
HEC LEEMA

# FILMS & SERIES IN AND ABOUT ANTWERP

**Snatch (2000)**

Directed by Guy Ritchie, *Snatch* is a British crime comedy film (with Brad Pitt, Jason Statham, and Vinnie Jones) set in London but featuring various international characters. The story revolves around a series of interconnected events involving diamond theft, illegal boxing, and organised crime. Antwerp plays a significant role as it is one of the locations where a valuable diamond is traded and stolen, setting off a chain of chaotic events.

**Any Way the Wind Blows (2003)**

Tom Barman, frontman of the famous Belgian rock band dEUS, directed the Flemish film *Any Way the Wind Blows*. The film, set in Antwerp on a day in June, follows the intertwining lives of eight characters, each dreaming about a different life.

**De Zaak Alzheimer (2003), Memory (2022)**

*De Zaak Alzheimer* (The Alzheimer Affair) is a Belgian thriller about the best Antwerp detective duo who investigate the murder of a high-ranking official. The detectives do everything in their power to catch the perpetrator (who appears to suffer from Alzheimer's), and as they delve deeper into the investigation, they uncover a web of dark secrets, betrayal, and corruption. In 2022, its Hollywood remake titled Memory was released, starring Liam Neeson, Guy Pearce, and Monica Bellucci.

### Loft (2008), The Loft (2014)

In the film *Loft*, five married men share a loft where they can engage in extramarital affairs. However, their secret sanctuary becomes a crime scene when a woman's dead body is discovered, leading to suspicion and betrayal among the friends. *The Loft* (2014) is an American remake. Antwerp serves as the primary setting for both films, providing the urban backdrop of the loft's location and the setting of much of their suspenseful action.

### Cordon (2014)

The outbreak of a deadly virus in Antwerp prompts authorities to quarantine a section of the city to avoid its spread. The series *Cordon* explores the social, political, and personal consequences of the quarantine as people struggle to survive and maintain order.

### Zillion (2022)

The film *Zillion* is centred around the famous former Antwerp nightclub. It explores the cultural significance and legacy of the club, delving into its rise, heyday, and decline. Antwerp is integral to the storyline as the city where Zillion was located, showcasing its influence on the local nightlife scene.

### The Antwerp Diamond Heist (2023)

This short documentary, narrated by Pierce Brosnan, chronicles the infamous diamond heist that took place in Antwerp. It explores the details of the robbery, the perpetrators involved, and the subsequent investigations and fallout. Antwerp is the primary setting for the documentary, as the diamond heist occurred within the city's diamond district.

GOOD LUCK TO YOU,
LEO GRANDE
BLUE JEAN
PAWLIKOWSKI
WAR
SOLAR
AGNES V.
SWANN ARLA

**Fubar (2023)**

*Fubar* is a Netflix series which is partly set in Antwerp. You will see Arnold Schwarzenegger as a CIA agent racing the streets of the city centre in a sports car, and drinking the local De Koninck beer, or *Bolleke*.

**Rough Diamonds (2023)**

Belgian actor Kevin Janssens appears in the Netflix series *Rough Diamonds,* in which the main character travels back to his hometown of Antwerp after the suicide of his younger brother. He reconnects with the community he abandoned when he left the Orthodox Jewish faith. Back home, he tries to save his family's diamond business under the pressure from the underworld.

**Everybody Loves Diamonds (2023)**

Italian TV series *Everybody Loves Diamonds* follows a team of small-time Italian thieves who manage to deceive top-level security to steal millions of dollars' worth of precious stones from the Antwerp Diamond Centre.

# BOOKS IN & ABOUT ANTWERP

### A Dog of Flanders – Marie Louise de la Ramée

Set in 19th century Antwerp, this 1872 classic novel tells the heart-warming story of a young boy named Nello and his faithful dog, Patrasche. Despite facing poverty and hardship, Nello dreams of becoming an artist. The novel explores themes of friendship, loyalty, and the power of art. Against the backdrop of Antwerp's picturesque landscapes and vibrant culture, their tale unfolds, touching the hearts of readers for generations.

### Het dwaallicht (Will o' the Wisp) – Willem Elsschot

This 1946 novella by Willem Elsschot, one of Belgium's most celebrated authors, is set in Antwerp. It follows the protagonist Laarmans as he encounters three mysterious characters one foggy November evening. The story takes readers on a nocturnal journey through the streets of Antwerp, exploring themes of loneliness, chance encounters, and existential questions. As Laarmans navigates the city's labyrinthine alleys and encounters various characters, including a lost sailor and a young girl, the novella captures the atmosphere and spirit of Antwerp, revealing its darker side.

### Austerlitz – W.G. Sebald

Set in various European cities, including Antwerp, the 2001 book *Austerlitz* is a heartfelt and haunting novel that delves into themes of memory, identity, and the impact of history. Protagonist Jacques Austerlitz recounts his quest to uncover his own mysterious past, leading him to

↓ WILLEM ELSSCHOT BY DICK MATENA

Antwerp, among other places. It is the incredible story of a man who was robbed of his homeland, his language and his name as a child, and who no longer fits into this world.

### Wil (Will) – Jeroen Olyslaegers

Set during World War II in Nazi-occupied Antwerp, *Wil* follows the protagonist, Wilfried Wils, as he navigates the moral complexities of survival, collaboration, and resistance. Against the backdrop of a city under siege, Wilfried struggles with his own choices and loyalty, torn between self-preservation and his conscience. In his 2016 novel, Olyslaegers masterfully captures the atmosphere of fear and betrayal in wartime Antwerp.

**Wildevrouw – Jeroen Olyslaegers**
---

In his 2020 historical novel, Olyslaegers explores Antwerp's tumultuous period in the 16th century. The story revolves around the main character, Beer, who lost three wives in childbirth, after which he looks back on his time in Antwerp. Against the backdrop of religious turmoil and social disorder, the story follows the lives of various characters, including artists, rebels, and nobles, whose fates intertwine amidst the scenery of 16th century Antwerp. In Dutch only.

**Het stad in mij – Maud Vanhauwaert**
---

This collection of two years of Antwerp poetry (2018 – 2019) by city poet Maud Vanhauwaert explores the city through the lens of personal reflection and introspection. *Het stad in mij* (The city in me) is a combination of poetry in words and images, incorporated in an experimental and conceptually designed book. In Dutch only.

**'t Stad van vroeger – Tanguy Ottomer**
---

Written by local historian and tour guide Tanguy Ottomer, *'t Stad van vroeger* (The city of the past) takes readers on a nostalgic journey through the history of Antwerp. Through archival photographs, anecdotes, and historical insights, Ottomer illuminates the city's past, tracing its evolution from ancient times to present day. In Dutch only.

**Antwerp: The Glory Years – Michael Pye**

Authored by English historian Michael Pye in 2021, *Antwerp: The Glory Years* chronicles Antwerp during the 16th century. Pye explores the city's rise as a centre of commerce, art, and culture, tracing its flourishing trade, influential artists, and vibrant society. From the majestic architecture of its guild halls to the masterpieces of its painters, the book celebrates Antwerp's cultural heritage and its enduring legacy as a beacon of creativity and innovation.

**Historical Atlas of Antwerp – various authors**

This historical atlas, with the subtitle 'Between Aspiration and Achievement', published in 2022, offers a visual exploration of Antwerp's past, tracing its development from ancient times to the present day. Through maps, illustrations, and informative text, the atlas provides insights into the city's urban layout, architectural landmarks, and significant historical events. From its strategic location as a trading hub to its cultural contributions and societal transformations, the atlas offers a nuanced perspective on Antwerp's dynamic history.

**De geuren van de kathedraal – Wendy Wauters**

*De geuren van de kathedraal* (The scents of the cathedral) is a 2023 novel set in Antwerp that explores the intertwined lives of various characters against the backdrop of the city's iconic cathedral. Through sensory-rich prose and detailed storytelling, Wauters delves into the hustle and bustle of the cathedral. Get to know its visitors from many walks of life and its remarkable sounds and smells, where religious serenity was sometimes hard to find. In Dutch only.

# FUN FACTS

### Sinjoren

People born in Antwerp are affectionately known as *Sinjoren*, a term derived from the Spanish word *señor*, reflecting the historical influence of Spanish rule in the region. The nickname has two definitions. Some consider only those whose parents and ancestors were born in Antwerp as Sinjoor. Others only speak of a 'true' Sinjoor if they were born within the Spanish Fortress, located between De Leien and the Scheldt.

### First Stock Exchange

Antwerp established the world's first stock exchange in 1531, marking a crucial moment in the evolution of global financial markets. In the 16th century, this 'mother of all stock exchanges' served as a model for many others in Europe. The powerful monument completely burned down in 1583 and in 1858, only to rise from its ashes again and again.

### Diamond Trade Hub

Approximately 80% of the world's uncut diamonds transit through Antwerp, underscoring its status as a premier diamond trading centre and making it the diamond capital of the world. Next to Antwerpen-Centraal, you will find the Diamond Square Mile, home to diamond cutters, jewellers, and diamond dealers. The inventor of the brilliant cut was a 19-year-old Antwerp resident who discovered the mathematical formula to cut a diamond in such a way that it could shine to maximum effect in 1919.

**Coffee Storage Capital**

Antwerp houses the world's largest coffee storage facility, capable of accommodating a staggering equivalent of 43 billion cups of coffee, highlighting its key role in the coffee trade. Antwerp also has the largest number of coffee bars in Belgium, so your daily cup of joe is never far away.

**Oldest Skyscraper in Europe**

The iconic 1932 *Boerentoren* (Farmers' Tower) stands as one of Europe's oldest skyscrapers, symbolising Antwerp's rich architectural heritage. To this day it remains a beautiful example of Art Deco in the city. At a height of 97 metres, it is the third tallest tower in Antwerp.

### Nello & Patrasche

To honour the touching and world-famous Antwerp tale of poor orphan boy Nello and his loyal stray dog Patrasche (see page xxx), their statue by Batist Vermeulen serves as a beloved landmark in front of the Onze-Lieve-Vrouwekathedraal. The lovely, inseparable couple has been resting in an embrace under a blanket of cobblestones since 2016.

### Koekenstad (Cookie City)

Between 1830 and 1960, more than twenty large biscuit and chocolate factories were present in Antwerp, giving it the sweet nickname of *Koekenstad*.

### Antwerpse Handjes

The delicious regional product *Antwerpse Handjes* (Antwerp Hands) are hand-shaped biscuits or chocolates. These little hands are a reference to the myth of the hand of Antigoon (see page xx).

### Boot Scrapers

Throughout Antwerp, boot scrapers (once used to scrape off mud and horse dung from boots before entering a house) have been transformed into cute miniature scenes by Elke Lemmens of Hausgemacht, adding a playful charm to the cityscape. By scanning the QR-code next to these scrapers, you'll discover the stories behind these miniature worlds. Or use the *Street Art Cities* app to find them all.

### Madonna statues

As Mary is the patron saint of Antwerp, she appears on many façades and corners of houses. In a total of 170 places throughout the city, actually. They were installed at the end of the 17th century and early in the 18th century, and often served as street lighting, as many statues were equipped with an oil lamp. Don't forget to look up: you can spot her everywhere. Behind St. Paulus Church, there even is a Lourdes Grotto to be found.

↓ NELLO & PATRASCHE: A STORY OF FRIENDSHIP BY BATIST VERMEULEN

# PHOTO SPOTS

**Centraal Station**

*Koningin Astridplein 27, Centrum*

Antwerpen-Centraal is more than just a transportation hub; it's a symphony of movement frozen in time. Photograph the station's iconic dome amidst the flurry of commuters, capturing the intersection of architecture and human activity. Opt for long exposure shots to evoke a sense of dynamic energy or wait for the golden hour to cast a warm glow upon its impressive façade.

**Chinatown**

*Van Wesenbekestraat, Centrum*

Antwerp's Chinatown is a kaleidoscope of colours, flavours, and traditions waiting to be immortalised through your lens. Wander through its bustling street lined with red streetlights and decorated façades, capturing candid moments of daily life. Embrace the vibrant colours of the restaurants and supermarkets, and the detailed Chinese gateway for unique photographic opportunities.

**Handelsbeurs**

*Twaalfmaandenstraat 9, Centrum, handelsbeursantwerpen.be*

Nestled within Antwerp's heart, Handelsbeurs exudes an aura of timeless elegance. Capture its grandeur by framing its complex architectural details, and hand-painted world maps. Experiment with different angles to highlight its majestic roof with its neo-Gothic iron roof construction and play with lighting to accentuate its arcades. Only open at weekends.

↓ CENTRAAL STATION

↓ MAS

Een goed stadsgedicht
herkent u meteen.
Het heeft een rake titel,
opent gevat,
en in het beste geval
hangt het in de weg
aan de onderkant van
een enorme brug.

Het is grappig,
maar niet overdreven.

En het verrast
— op de valreep
stelt het dan toch nog iets
zoals bijvoorbeeld
de ellendige vraag:

Vervoert dit schip
niet arg rustig de tijd
die u hier zo dringend
staat te verliezen?

Een goed
stadsgedicht
Stijn Vranken

**Vlaeykensgang**

*Oude Koornmarkt 16 / Pelgrimstraat 4, Centrum*

Step into the charming Vlaeykensgang walk through its narrow passages and hidden corners, and capture the timeless beauty of its medieval architecture. Experiment with low-light photography to capture the atmospheric glow of lanterns and (sometimes) candlelit windows in the evening.

**Felix Pakhuis**

*Godefriduskaai 30, North*

Built in the 1860s, Felix Pakhuis was a warehouse for bulk goods such as coffee, wheat, sugar, and tobacco. Explore its spacious interior with the weathered iron doors, white brickwork, and glass roof construction. Experiment with shadows and highlights to accentuate its architectural features and consider shooting during the golden hour to infuse your images with a soft, elegant glow.

**Havenhuis**

*Zaha Hadidplein 1, North, portofantwerpbruges.com*

Like a futuristic ship emerging from the water, Havenhuis (the Port Authority Building) commands attention with its avant-garde design. Explore its angular contours and reflective surfaces to capture its allure. Experiment with reflections to create mesmerizing compositions and consider shooting at twilight to emphasise its modernity against the waterscape of Antwerp's port.

**MAS Rooftop Panorama**

*Hanzestedenplaats 1, North, mas.be*

Ascend to the MAS rooftop for a free panoramic perspective of Antwerp's skyline, where the city's rhythm unfolds beneath you. Frame the architectural mosaic of rooftops against the vast expanse of sky and play with perspective to create a sense of depth and dimension. Experiment with different focal lengths to capture both sweeping vistas and small details, and don't forget to include the Scheldt River as an attractive leading line.

**Old Cranes**

*Rijnkaai 150, North*

The old cranes at Waagnatie stand as silent guardians of Antwerp's maritime heritage and centuries of trade. Capture their weathered elegance against the backdrop of the Scheldt, experimenting with framing to emphasise their towering presence. Consider shooting from unique viewpoints to highlight their old machinery and textures and embrace the play of light and shadow to create a sense of nostalgia.

**Parkbrug**

*Italiëlei 9, North*

Parkbrug exemplifies modern urban design. Frame its sleek lines against the green backdrop of Park Spoor Noord, capturing the symphony of cyclists and pedestrians. Experiment with long exposure photography to blur motion and create a sense of dynamic energy. And when the sun is shining, you will be treated to a beautiful interplay of shadows!

**PAKT**

*Regine Beerplein 1, East/South, www.pakt-antwerpen.be*

A living canvas where creativity thrives amidst industrial charm. Explore PAKT's repurposed warehouses with artisanal cafés and restaurants, capturing the meeting of innovation and heritage. Experiment with framing to mix modern design elements with rustic textures. From April to October, you can regularly visit the roof garden with a guide. It's the perfect place to capture a serene green oasis with the city as a backdrop.

PHOTO SPOTS

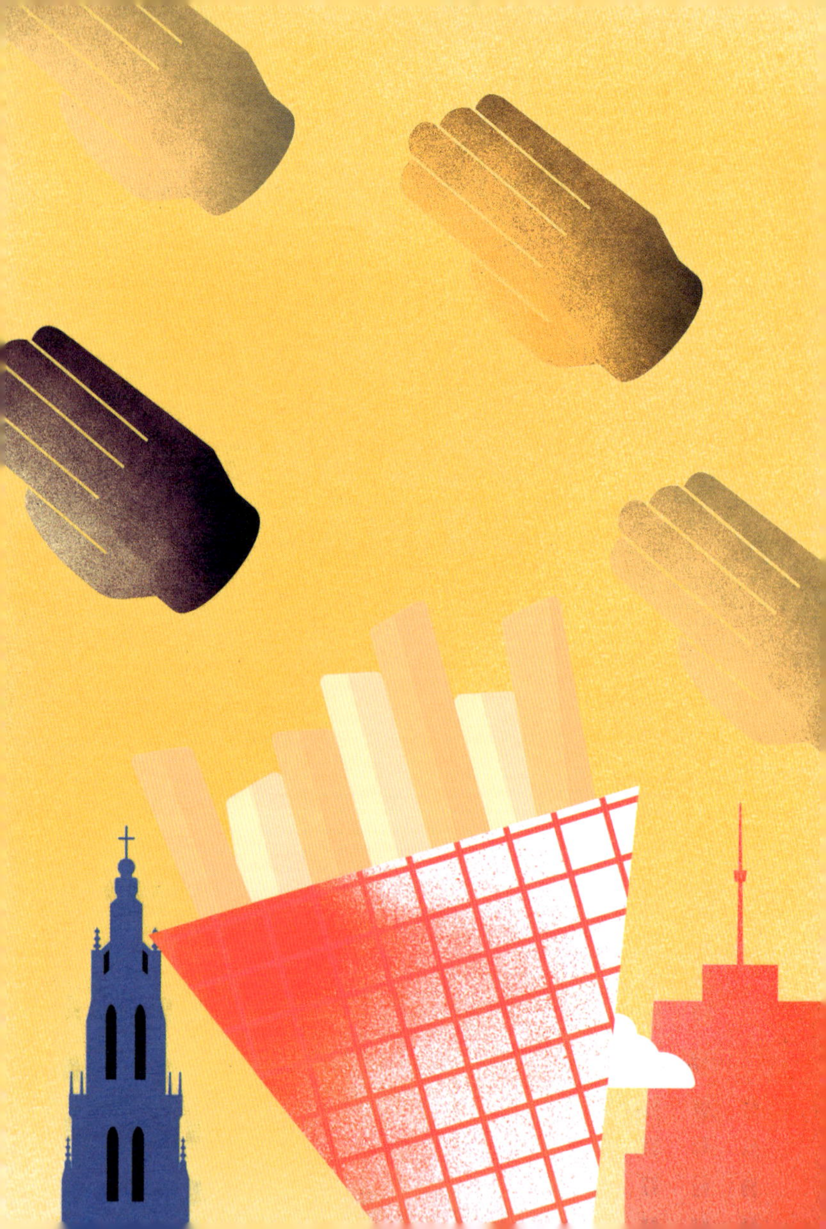

# FOOD AND DRINKS

# COFFEE & TEA

### Caffènation

Probably the most renowned name in the Antwerp specialty coffee scene, Caffènation has four locations across the city. Whether it's the bustling CITY location or the more relaxed PAKT site, you can expect a superb coffee experience at any Caffènation spot. They also have an extensive range of home baked cookies and pastries, which varies a bit per location. Vegans should check out KOCO, because they offer everything plant-based.

*caffenation.be*

### Caffe Mundi

With its inviting ambiance, Caffe Mundi is a cosy coffee shop with a cushy interior. The baristas use freshly roasted beans from their own roastery next door and ensure that each cup is brewed to perfection. There is also a small breakfast/lunch menu and lots of home-baked cakes. As soon as the weather allows it, their terrace is filled in no time.

*Oude Beurs 24, Centrum, caffemundi.be*

### Normo

Normo is a specialty coffee shop with their own roastery. The atmosphere of this vintage-style coffee bar is very relaxed and laid-back. Don't fancy a coffee? Their hot chocolate is great as well, especially in winter, with a good dollop of whipped cream.

*Minderbroedersrui 30, Centrum, normocoffee.be*

### Black and Yellow

A no-nonsense coffee spot with good vibes, great (hip-hop) tunes, and a very strong community of regulars. Owner Joke sources premium beans from Belgian and Dutch roasters. The pavement terrace is popular with locals for socialising and soaking up the sun.

*Nassaustraat 7, North, blackandyellowcoffee.com*

### Kūkai

From classic matcha lattes to innovative matcha-infused creations such as cashew matcha latte and coconut water matcha, each drink at Kūkai is carefully made using high-quality matcha imported straight from Japan. Kūkai also offers a selection of sweets to complement the rich and earthy matcha flavours.

*Falconplein 37, North, kukai.studio*

### RUSH RUSH

Aeropress lovers should definitely visit RUSH RUSH, as owner Simon won first place in the 2018 and 2022 Belgian Aeropress Championships and second place in the 2022 World Championships. Other than specialty coffee and tea, they also serve a small breakfast/lunch menu, including delicious homemade cakes and pastries. Owners Nanigui and Simon prioritise on traceable, seasonal, high-quality coffee with great flavours for their own roastery in the Antwerp suburbs.

*Lange Altaarstraat 29, East, rushrush.be*

### Andy Roasters

The energetic and funky Andy specialty coffee shop spun off from the well-known cafe Butchers Coffee. At Andy, they carefully select high-quality coffee beans from around the world, which they give a light roast. Their blends have chocolaty, nutty notes while their selection of single origin coffees have fruity, more complex notes. In the back you'll find a record shop, and in the front a busy and lively terrace, often overflowing with sunshine.

*Amerikalei 82, South, andy-roasters.be*

### Butchers Coffee

As the name Butchers Coffee and its logo (a hook) suggests, this coffee shop is housed in a former butcher's shop. It's a unique coffee spot with a strong passion for the community. Owner Dave has brought a distinct Australian flair to Butcher's Coffee, drawing on his five years of barista experience in Melbourne. The terrace, with its long wooden tables and benches, is the perfect spot for larger groups. In 2020, the owners started their own roastery called Andy Roasters, which now has its own coffee shop just a five-minute walk away.

*Kasteelstraat 57, South, butcherscoffee.be*

# BAKERIES

### Bakker Aldo

Bakker Aldo bakes delicious bread, made with a sourdough starter that has been passed down through generations. Besides bread, they offer a variety of perfectly baked goods like croissants, cinnamon buns, pastries, and cakes, with a focus on quality ingredients. Discover these delicacies in the vaulted ground floor of a former city archive called Het Archief.

*Geefsstraat 5, Centrum, inhetarchief.be*

### Bakkerij Goossens

Since 1884, Bakkerij Goossens has been known for their freshly baked pastries and bread, perfect for a morning treat or afternoon snack. This beautiful traditional bakery is a feast for the eyes and a popular place for many locals. It's tiny, which means there often is a queue outside, but don't let that put you off. You just must try their *roggeverdommeke*, a typical Antwerp rye bread enriched with currants, raisins, and butter.

*Korte Gasthuisstraat 31, Centrum*

### Bakkerij FUNK

At this vegan bakery, you can get a cup of coffee in the morning and a glass of natural wine in the afternoon. The range of pastries at Bakkerij FUNK changes weekly, but some classics are always available. For those with a craving for something savoury, they also serve sourdough toasts. This 'funky' place is very popular, so you may have to wait a while to get a spot. It is worth the wait!

*Kronenburgstraat 41A, South, insta @bakkerijfunk*

# BREAKFAST & LUNCH

### Oats Day Long

Brother Ewout and sister Anse took oatmeal to the next level when they opened the first oatmeal bar of the region. They wondered why you would eat oatmeal for breakfast only, when it's enjoyable all day long? Oats Day Long creates breakfast bowls (açaí, matcha, lemon poppy, banana), pancakes, bagels, and sandwiches with several toppings at two locations in the city. Finish your breakfast or lunch with one of their organic juices or smoothies and you're good to go.

*oatsdaylong.be*

VEDETT
SUGGESTIE:
frisse
PARELCOUSCOUS
met groenten en
TOPPING naar keuze
-kip
-rosbief
-mozzarella
geitenkaas
Let the
FUN TIMES
BE
GIN
istro Theo_FREE-WIFI
€24,-
TAKE YOUR BOTTLE HOME
UP
serranoham

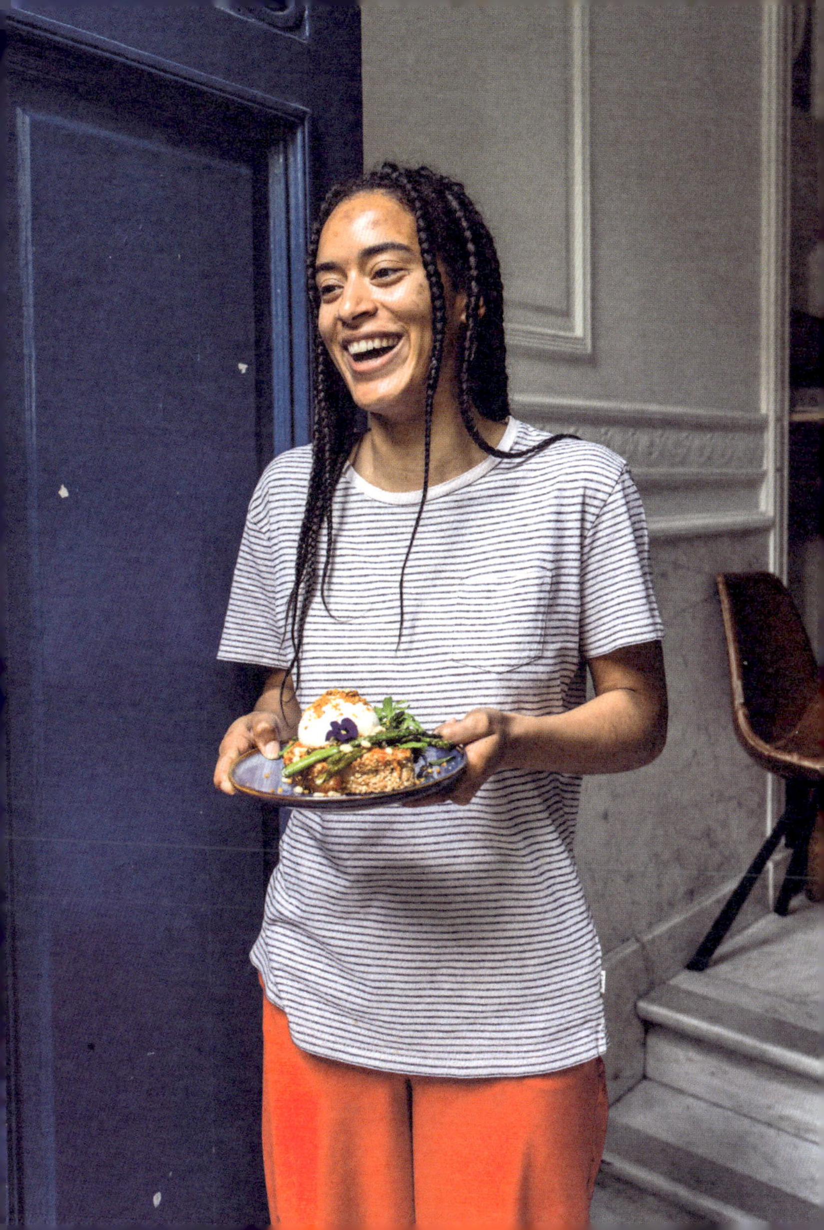

## Charlie's Antwerpen

Whether you have a small appetite or are very hungry, start your day with one of four different breakfast options, ranging from a croissant with scrambled eggs, to the Charlie's Deluxe Breakfast with everything your heart desires. This inviting place also offers toasts, salads, and delicious homemade desserts. Any dish can be prepared gluten free.

*Volkstraat 66, South, charliesantwerpen.be*

↓ NORDICA 31

## Barnini

Barnini is a popular coffee spot and bagel shop that exudes a vibrant and eclectic charm. The menu features a selection of sweet treats and lots of savoury bagel creations. The cheerful ambiance, the quirky decor and the wonderful terrace create a welcoming atmosphere.

*Oudevaartplaats 10, Centrum, insta @barnini_the_bagelclub*

↓ BLACK AND YELLLOW

### Cafématic

Cafématic is the go-to place for breakfast and lunch with modern classics like eggs benedict, sourdough with hummus, BLT toast, and goat's cheese salad. There is something for everyone on their menu, including homemade cold drinks, juices, and all kinds of (non) alcoholic drinks. The setting is very relaxed and their outdoor terrace hugely popular.

*Vleminckveld 4, Centrum, insta @ cafematicantwerpen*

### Exotische Markt & Vogelmarkt

Every Saturday and Sunday you can indulge in traditional Belgian dishes as well as world cuisines at the *Exotische Markt* ('exotic market') and *Vogelenmarkt* ('bird market'). Many market stalls serve a variety of affordable lunch options, including classic Belgian croquettes, Vietnamese spring rolls, Thai stir-fry dishes, Turkish wraps, and everything in between. The locals like to meet each other to enjoy the delicious food paired with a glass of wine, beer or champagne. No matter the cold, it is always bustling, with a very pleasant and lively vibe. Rain might throw a spanner in the works, though.

*Exotische Markt: Saturday 8am – 4pm,*
*Vogelmarkt: Sunday 8am – 1 or 2pm*
*(weather dependent)*
*Oude Vaartplaats / Theaterplein, Centrum*

### Kaffeenini

With a large outdoor terrace, Kaffeenini is a charming coffee shop and bagel joint. It is known for its array of sweet treats and freshly baked bagels. The menu boasts a variety of bagel creations, ranging from classic combinations to innovative flavour pairings, satisfying both savoury and sweet cravings.

*Nationalestraat 114A, Centrum ,*
*kaffeenini.be*

### Tinsel

With their slogan 'no muss, no fuss', good vibes are guaranteed. Tinsel is known for its creative breakfast and lunch options, including oats, pancakes, toasts, and sandwiches. Start your day in its cosy and stylish restaurant with a delicious breakfast or enjoy the afternoon hours with some lunch or *apéro*. When the sun is out, their terrace is a desired spot.

*Sint-Paulusplaats 30, North, tinsel.be*

### Quite Frankly

When you cross the threshold of Quite Frankly, you immediately feel like you are in a real American diner. Grab a stool at the counter and enjoy classics like buttermilk pancakes, biscuits and gravy, Philly Cheesesteak, home-made pastrami, a Rueben Sandwich, or Sloppy Joe. Expect generous portions; you certainly won't be leaving hungry.

*Klapdorp 57, North, quitefrankly.be*

### Walvis

Walvis is a versatile lunch spot that serves up a fusion of modern Mediterranean, Middle Eastern, and Asian flavours. Here you can start the day with granola or eggs prepared in various ways. For lunch you can choose between toasties, soup, noodle salad, tacos or shakshuka, to name a few.

*Walvisstraat 1, East, walvisantwerpen.com*

### Nordica 31

While travelling in Scandinavian and Nordic countries, a love for their cuisine was sparked in owner Lisa. Nordica 31 is known for some of the best cardamom and cinnamon buns in town, while offering a *hygge* atmosphere. For breakfast, they'll offer toast, waffles, *skyr*, oats, or a full Nordic breakfast. Or have lunch with homemade brioche, salads, or *smørrebrød* with homemade Danish rye

↓ CHARLIE'S ANTWERPEN

bread. Dishes are seasoned in the typical Nordic way, with pickled union, beetroot, cucumber, cranberry sauce, and sour cream.

*Belegstraat 31, East/South, nordica31.be*

### Racine PAKT

In the creative PAKT area, Racine provides a fresh and wholesome food experience with several types of sandwiches and salads for lunch. Sweet treats are served all day, and for Sundays, they have a separate brunch menu. Their lush roof terrace offers great views over the former industrial warehouses.

*Lamorinièrestraat 161, East/South, racinepakt.be*

### Vers Zuid

The name Vers (fresh) says it all, go there for sandwiches and salads made with the freshest ingredients. The options are numerous with about twenty types of sandwiches, ten different salads, a wide choice of hot sandwiches, several homemade soups, and some hot and cold dishes. Think pasta, lasagna, moussaka, quinoa bowls, grilled vegetables, and meatballs. It's a very convenient spot for a quick and tasty lunch.

*Kloosterstraat 187, South, verszuid.be*

# FRIETEN (CHIPS)

### CHIPS

A top destination for lovers of this fried delicacy, Chips is serving up crispy delights with a variety of homemade items, like a Flemish jackfruit stew or chicken satay. An abundance of vegan and vegetarian snacks, burgers and sauces is available to choose from as well.

*Sint-Antoniusstraat 35, Centrum, chips.be*

### Frites Atelier

Known for its gourmet chips, Frites Atelier presents a modern twist on the Belgian classic. In addition to rotating specials, there are always some classics on the menu, like parmesan & basil, Flemish stew, and Indonesian peanut. Their chips are seasoned with salt extracted from samphire, a plant that thrives in saltwater environments.

*Korte Gasthuisstraat 32, Centrum, fritesatelier.com*

# DINNER

### Boker Tov

Specialising in Tel Aviv recipes, Boker Tov gives a taste of the region's vibrant food scene. At all three locations breakfast is served all day, or have lunch with a pastrami sandwich, chicken wrap, sourdough pita, *labneh*, falafel, hummus, *muhammara*, or *shakshuka*. Hard to choose? Then go for the *Balagan Experience*, a selection of dishes for two.

*bokertov.be*

### Little Bún

Little Bún serves authentic Vietnamese street food, including fresh dishes like rice noodles with several toppings, pho noodle soup, and rice paper rolls. You can find them in the neighbourhoods of Eilandje (North) and Het Zuid.

*bunantwerp.be*

### Pici

Indulge in fresh, homemade pasta dishes inspired by Italian culinary traditions at one of the two Pici locations in town. Enjoy their authentic flavours and comforting classics, but always leave room for dessert. The best way to end your meal is with a creamy tiramisu, panna cotta or Italian gelato.

*pastapici.be*

### Takumi

Craving hearty ramen? Takumi is the best in authentic Japanese Sapporo ramen,

SAPPORO RAMEN KITCHEN
TAKUMI
麺処
SAPPORO RAMEN
匠
-TAKUMI-
RAMEN KITCHEN
TAKUMI
ANTWERPEN
YUGIRI SANJYURO

serving up steaming bowls of flavourful broth, noodles, and toppings. The atmosphere adds to the dining experience, transporting diners to the streets of Japan. There are five locations across the city with an overlapping menu, but often with a certain specialty for each. For example: Tonkotsu Ramen at Grote Markt (Centrum), Yakisoba at Groenplaats (Centrum), or Chicken Ramen at Marnixplaats (South).

*takumiramennoodles.com*

### Alma Libre

Experience the taste of Mexico at Alma Libre, where they serve delicious tacos filled with a variety of flavourful ingredients such as juicy pulled pork, chicken mole, and spicy refried beans. Crispy nachos, enchiladas, burritos, and empanadas are also on the menu.

*Scheldestraat 42, Centrum, almalibre.be*

### Balls & Glory

Feast on homemade meatballs, served with a variety of sauces and sides. The menu of Balls & Glory offers a range of creative flavour combinations to satisfy meat lovers and vegetarians alike. As a side dish, you can choose a typical Belgian *stoemp* (a mash made of potato, carrot, peas, and butter) or a salad.

*Theaterplein 1, Centrum, ballsnglory.be*

### Bia Mara

For fans of fish and chips, Bia Mara is serving up crispy battered sustainable fish alongside hand-cut chips and a variety of flavourful sauces. There is also a choice of tacos (fish, chicken or squid) and burgers (fish, chicken or halloumi).

*Maalderijstraat 1, Centrum, biamara.com*

### Camino

Infused with Asian inspiration, Camino introduces dishes influenced by the authentic

↓ FRITES ATELIER

flavours of East and Southeast Asia. From sushi rolls to noodle bowls and dumplings, there's something for every palate on the menu, which changes weekly.

*Muntstraat 4, Centrum, caminoantwerp.com*

### In de Roscam

This homely bar at the charming Vrijdagmarkt offers a selection of sandwiches, soups, pasta dishes, and fresh salads. In de Roscam is a casual dining spot perfect for enjoying a leisurely meal or drink.

*Vrijdagmarkt 12, Centrum, roscam.cafe*

### Jean sur Mer

Jean sur Mer is a seafood-focused eatery offering a variety of fish snacks and street food. Here you can enjoy a homemade shrimp croquette, brioche burger (fish, crab, shrimp, beef, chicken or veggie), or fish and chips with a freshly pulled Belgian beer.

*Groenplaats 15, Centrum, jeansurmer.be*

### Kapitein Zeppos

In the rustic setting of Kapitein Zeppos, you can enjoy traditional Belgian classics such as hearty stews, *moules-frites* (mussels with fries), *vol-au-vents* (puff pastry filled with chicken and cream sauce), burgers, salads, and other regional specialties.

*Vleminckveld 78, Centrum, cafezeppos.be*

### Knees to Chin

For a fresh and delicious quick bite, indulge in rice paper rolls and other Asian street food at Knees to Chin. Their generously filled rolls are overflowing with sweet potato, omelette, minced chicken, satay tofu, or crispy bacon. Complete your lunch with a side, like a bowl of rice topped with peanut sauce, a cabbage salad or miso soup.

*Kammenstraat 29, Centrum, kneestochin.com*

## Plump

Plump has a menu filled with juicy smashed burgers made with high-quality beef, all topped with a variety of delicious ingredients. With its casual vibe and flavourful creations, Plump is a popular spot for indulging in satisfying comfort food.

*Kronenburgstraat 17, Centrum, plump.be*

## Satay

Specialising in Southeast Asian street food, Satay particularly focuses on satay skewers grilled to perfection and served with a variety of tasty sauces. The menu also features other Asian delicacies, like dumplings, *gado gado*, and roasted duck for a complete street-food experience.

*Wijngaardbrug 8, Centrum, satay.be*

**Via Via**

Via Via is more than just a restaurant; it's a meeting place for travellers to enjoy international cuisine together. With its vibrant atmosphere, it's a place where locals and visitors alike can gather to savour dishes from around the world while sharing travel stories and experiences.

*Wolstraat 43, Centrum, viavia.world*

**Mission Massala**

Explore a diverse menu of traditional Indian dishes bursting with aromatic spices and extensive tastes. From creamy curries to butter paneer to tandoori specialties, at Mission Massala you can experience the richness of Indian cuisine in a colourful and inviting setting.

*Dendermondestraat 68, East, missionmasala.be*

**Orso**

Orso caters to those with gluten sensitivities by offering a menu of delicious gluten-free pizzas. They are all made with fresh ingredients and flavourful toppings, like spicy pumpkin or king oyster mushrooms for example.

*Grote Beerstraat 46, East, orsopizzeria.be*

**Dabba King**

South Indian cuisine is known for its aromatic spices and tasty dishes. At Dabba King, you can savour mouth-watering fried lentil balls, *dosa* (savoury crêpes), several types of spicy curries, and the multi-layered flatbread *parotta*.

*Graaf van Egmontstraat 2, South, dabbaking.be*

**Dansing Chocola**

Blending the finest from Belgian and French cuisines, Dansing Chocola is your go-to for classic dishes.

From satisfying stews to crispy croquettes to delicate pastries, here you can experience the rich culinary traditions of both countries in a charming laid-back setting.

*Kloosterstraat 159, South*

**Finjan**

Focusing on Middle Eastern cuisine, Finjan is particularly known for its grilled meats and pita-based dishes. With their use of fresh ingredients and authentic spices, Finjan offers a taste of the Middle East through its delicious kebabs, shawarma, and mezze plates.

*Graaf van Hoornestraat 1, South, finjan.be*

**Sumac**

Sumac brings the vibrant flavours of Lebanese street food to Antwerp, offering a menu of traditional dishes such as mezze, falafel, köfte, *man'ousche* (a pizza grilled in the Josper oven), and grilled chicken with lemon and *za'atar*. With its lively atmosphere and bold seasoning, Sumac serves a taste of the bustling streets of Beirut.

*Vrijheidstraat 61, South, yumyum.world*

# BRING THE PARENTS

**Fiera**

You will be amazed by what might be the most beautiful restaurant in Antwerp. Fiera is located in the stunning 16th century Schippersbeurs (the former Shipping Exchange). Honest, carefully selected ingredients and worldly flavours adorn the menu, inspired by vibrant cities around the world.

*Lange Nieuwstraat 14, Centrum, fiera.be*

## DOJO 2.0

Discover modern Japanese cuisine in the heart of Antwerp's Meatpacking District. Be overwhelmed by their unique interior and attention to detail, while indulging in premium ingredients and pure flavours. Choose between floor seating (*horigotatsu*), table seating (*teburuseki*) or counter seating (*kauntaseki*) and go on an extraordinary culinary adventure.

*Samberstraat 7, North, do-jo.eu*

**Madonna Restaurant**

Dine surrounded by masterpieces at this restaurant inside the elegant Royal Museum of Fine Arts. Madonna's cuisine balances between rich tradition and delicious innovation. The chefs follow the rhythm of nature and use local and seasonal products to grace your plate.

*Leopold de Waelplaats 2, South, madonna-antwerp.be*

↓ FIERA

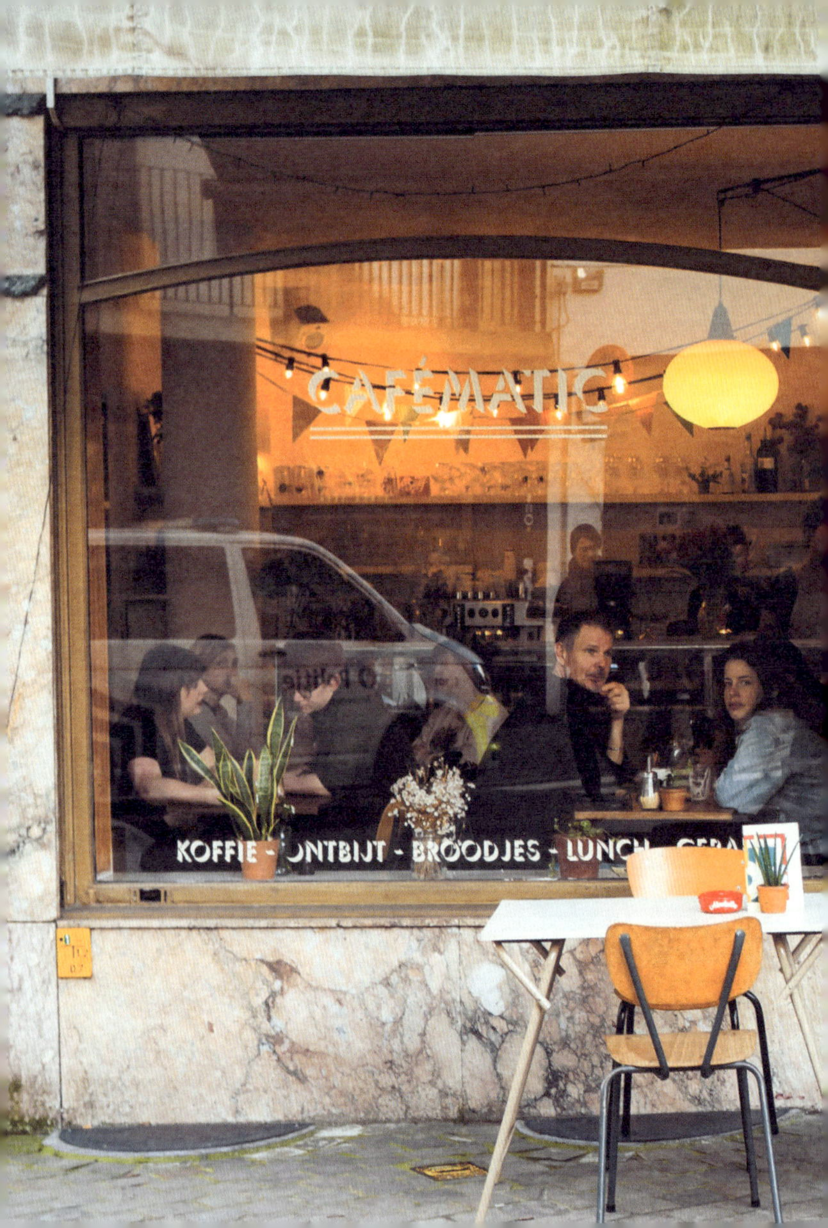
CAFÉMATIC
KOFFIE - ONTBIJT - BROODJES - LUNCH

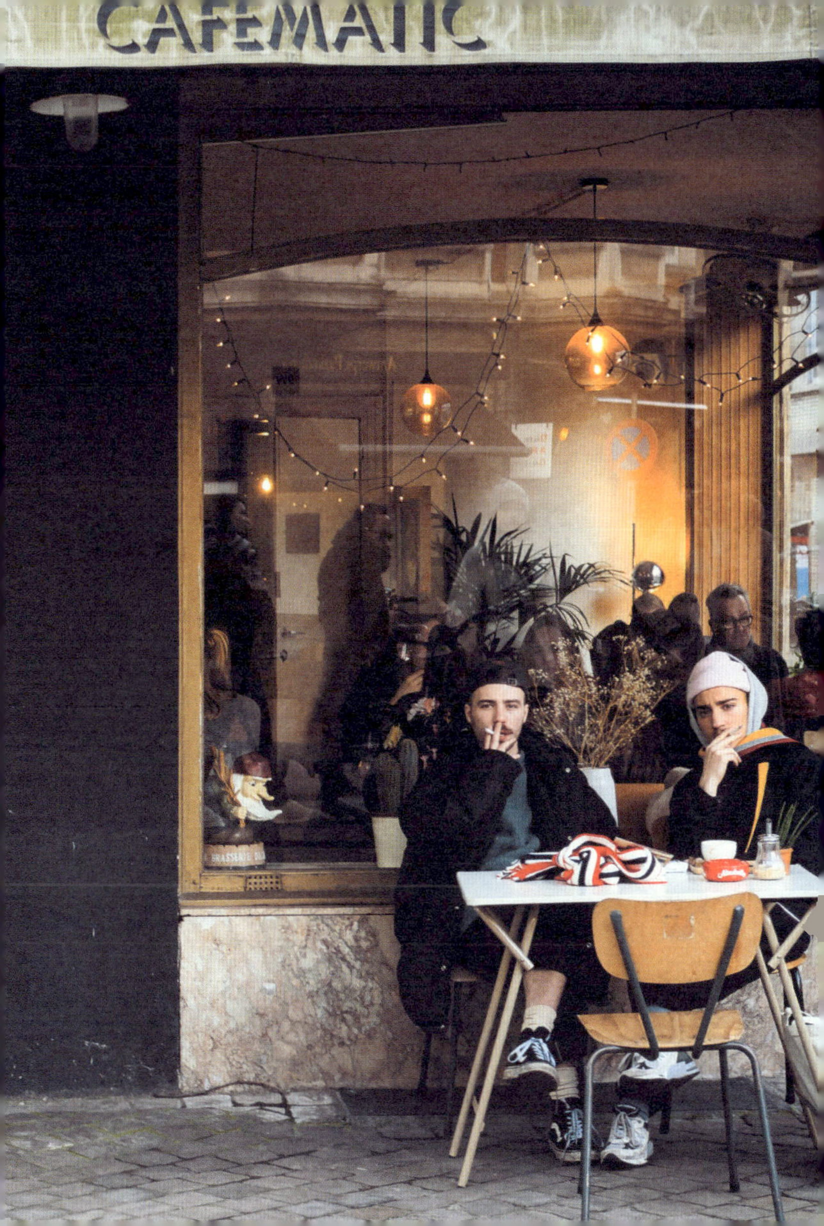
CAFEMATIC

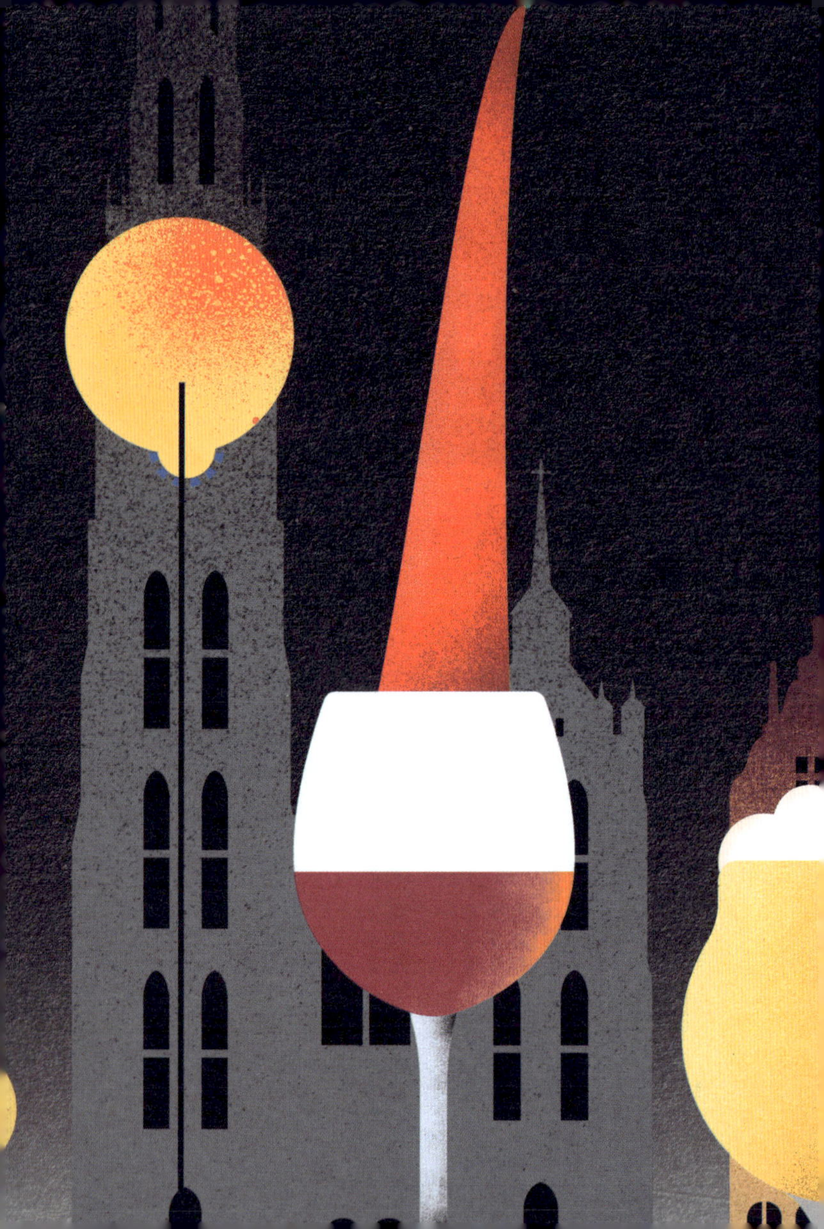

# GOING OUT

# BARS

**Beestenbos**

This neighbourhood bar has a homely feel. Its name Beestenbos (animal forest) refers to Toon Tellegen's fairy tales in which all animals, large and small, all know each other. The owners aim to achieve the same: creating a meeting place for young and old. Weekly concerts are held with some of Belgium's most talented musicians.

*Sint-Andriesplaats 17, Centrum, beestenbos.com*

**Korsakov**

In this retro bar you can feel a bit of a Berlin vibe, especially on the first floor with its pool table and graffiti-covered walls. If you get hungry after a few beers or wines, they serve excellent pub food, such as two types of pasta, pizzas, and daily specials.

*Sint-Jorispoort 1, Centrum, insta @korsakov_antwerp*

**De Muze**

Jazz lovers take note, this enchanting bar, boasting multiple floors of creaking wood, is your go-to spot for savouring drinks accompanied by soulful jazz melodies. Since 1964, this bar has been a permanent fixture for artists and creatives. Live concerts grace the stage of this 16th century building multiple times a week.

*Melkmarkt 15, Centrum, jazzcafedemuse.be*

**Tram 3**

Who would've guessed that behind this façade lies a quirky two-story bar with a rooftop terrace overlooking the cathedral? This is the ideal place for a party or an open mic evening with singing, poetry, music, or stand-up comedy. 'Lizzie o'clock' is occasionally announced via their socials: which means that at a specific hour their house beer Lizzie sells for just €2.50.

*Oude Koornmarkt 38, Centrum, tram-3.be*

**In Den Boer van Tienen**

Swing by Antwerp's second-oldest bar, serving up charm and drinks since around 1645. It's open daily from early morning until very late. During important sporting events, you can come here to watch the match while enjoying a draft beer.

*Mechelseplein 6, East, fb @indenboervantienen*

**Café Baron**

Located on the lively Marnixplaats, Café Baron has a casual atmosphere and reasonable prices. Their drinks menu is large, with nine beers on tap, about eight suggested beers, several *apéro* options, wines, cocktails and spirits. This place is always busy. Whenever the sun is out, their terrace is packed in no time.

*Marnixplaats 5, South, cafebaron.be*

**Café Vitrin**

On the other side of Marnixplaats, you'll find the energetic Café Vitrin, where creative locals meet. Arrive on time to assure a spot, because come rain or shine, every (terrace) seat gets filled at some point. They have their own beer called Vitsi, a bright blond beer, fresh with a touch of late hopping (Saaz).

*Marnixplaats 14, South, vitrincafe.com*

### Patine

The perfect spot for those seeking a French ambiance to savour a glass of wine, a fine pint, and bistro food. The evenings are pleasantly busy, particularly on the charming terrace with its atmospheric lights and a touch of Parisian flair.

*Leopold De Waelstraat 1, South gastro-by-mo.be/patine*

### Revista

At daytime, Revista is a lively café, perfect for a cup of coffee or lunch. But at night the atmosphere becomes even more dynamic when the crowds gather for *apéro* or drinks. On summer evenings a DJ often adds an extra party vibe on the terrace, but they are known to throw a good party inside too.

*Karel Rogierstraat 47, South, insta @ revista_antwerpen*

# QUEER

### Hessenhuis

Situated in a historic building that dates back to the 16th century, the Hessenhuis serves as a community hub where people can connect and support each other. Whether you are looking for a casual drink, a night out with friends or a place to celebrate your identity, this bar offers a warm and welcoming space for all.

*Falconrui 59, North, hessenhuis.be*

### Den Draak

Den Draak ('the dragon') is a straight-friendly gay bar in the beautiful Zurenborg neighbourhood. It is known as a warm, cosy, and atmospheric hangout. Keep an eye on their calendar for upcoming parties and events.

*Draakplaats 1, East, dendraak.be*

# COCKTAILS

## WINE

### Dogma

On multiple occasions, this informal speakeasy-style cocktail bar has been crowned the best in Europe. Immerse yourself in its warm retro-industrial interior, featuring inviting leather sofas and exposed brick walls. At Dogma, the spirit of the roaring twenties is revived.

*Wijngaardstraat 5, Centrum, dogmacocktails.be*

### Jones & Co

Nestled in the historical heart of Antwerp, Jones & Co is known for its intimate interior with a mezzanine and vaulted cellar. The menu features a wide selection of cocktails, including popular classics and inventive creations. On Wednesday evenings you will be treated to live performances.

*Pelgrimstraat 7, Centrum, jonesenco.be*

### Amber Bottle Shop

With an emphasis on quality and uniqueness, Amber provides an eclectic array of 400 natural wines. This wine bar has a bright and crisp interior with an energetic vibe. You can choose between Djuce canned wine, naturally sparkling, orange, and white or red wine.

*Schermersstraat 25, Centrum, amberbottleshop.com*

### Belgian Wines

The name says it all; here you can taste wines that are made exclusively from grapes grown in Belgium. The sommelier brothers who founded this wine bar and their enthusiastic employees can tell you everything about these Belgian vineyards and help you choose a wine to your liking. Especially recommended after visiting the Vogelenmarkt.

*Oudevaartplaats 24, Centrum, belgianwines.com*

### Titulus

The creative Titulus wine bar and cellar offers a selection of natural wines, liqueurs, sake, and natural alcohols. They have 200 wines in house, fifteen of which they serve by the glass. If you have your eye on one of the other 185 bottles, you'll pay a €10 corkage fee. In the evenings, they serve dishes from a small menu with a couple of mains and some small bites.

*Oever 8, Centrum, titulusantwerpen.be*

### Murukutum

Located on the lively Dageraadplaats, you will find the energetic Murukutum offering natural wines, craft beers, street food, with vinyl spinning on the record player. Experience a Caribbean feel with positive vibes in this colourful bar.

*Dageraadplaats 6, East, murukutum.be*

# CLUBS

### Club Capital

Club Capital is a basement dance and nightclub located in the lush Stadspark. Get ready to groove to disco, house, funk, and timeless dance classics.

*Rubenslei 37, Centrum, insta @clubcapital*

### Kasko

You will find Kasko, formerly known as Ampere, almost literally under the rumbling train tracks of Antwerpen-Centraal. It is a cultural and creative event space known for its underground nightlife experiences and concerts.

*Simonsstraat 21, Centrum, kasko.be*

### Cargo Club

In Antwerp's vibrant Red-Light District, Cargo Club is a permanent fixture for both straight and gay club-goers. With themed parties and a light and laser spectacle, there's always something exciting happening.

*Lange Schipperskapelstraat 11, North, cargoclub.be*

**Club Vaag**

Thursdays to Saturdays, Club Vaag becomes the epicentre for the celebration of techno and house. Stepping inside, you're enveloped by a symphony of lights and sounds, as DJs spin electrifying beats that resonate through the sleek, industrial-chic space.

*Rijnkaai 4, North, clubvaag.be*

**IKON Antwerpen**

At IKON, the nightlife scene ignites with a kaleidoscope of events, spanning across musical genres, from the pulsating rhythms of urban beats to the sounds of techno, and from dynamic hip-hop tunes to the adrenaline rush of drum & bass.

*Straatsburgdok Noordkaai 3, North, ikonantwerp.com*

**Plein Publiek**

DJs take the stage every Friday and Saturday night starting from 10.30pm at Plein Publiek. During the summer months, you can even go clubbing on their rooftop. Be sure to check the calendar for markets, live music, and other exciting events.

*Zonnestroomstraat 2, South, pleinpubliek.be*

↓ DOGMA

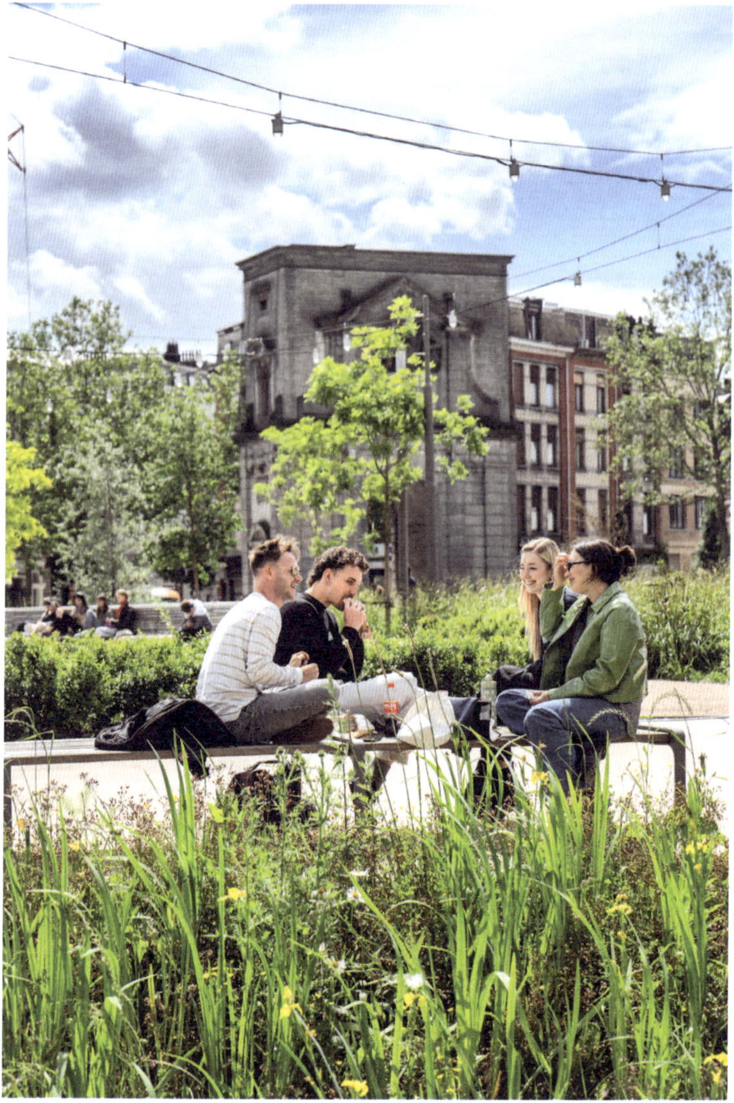

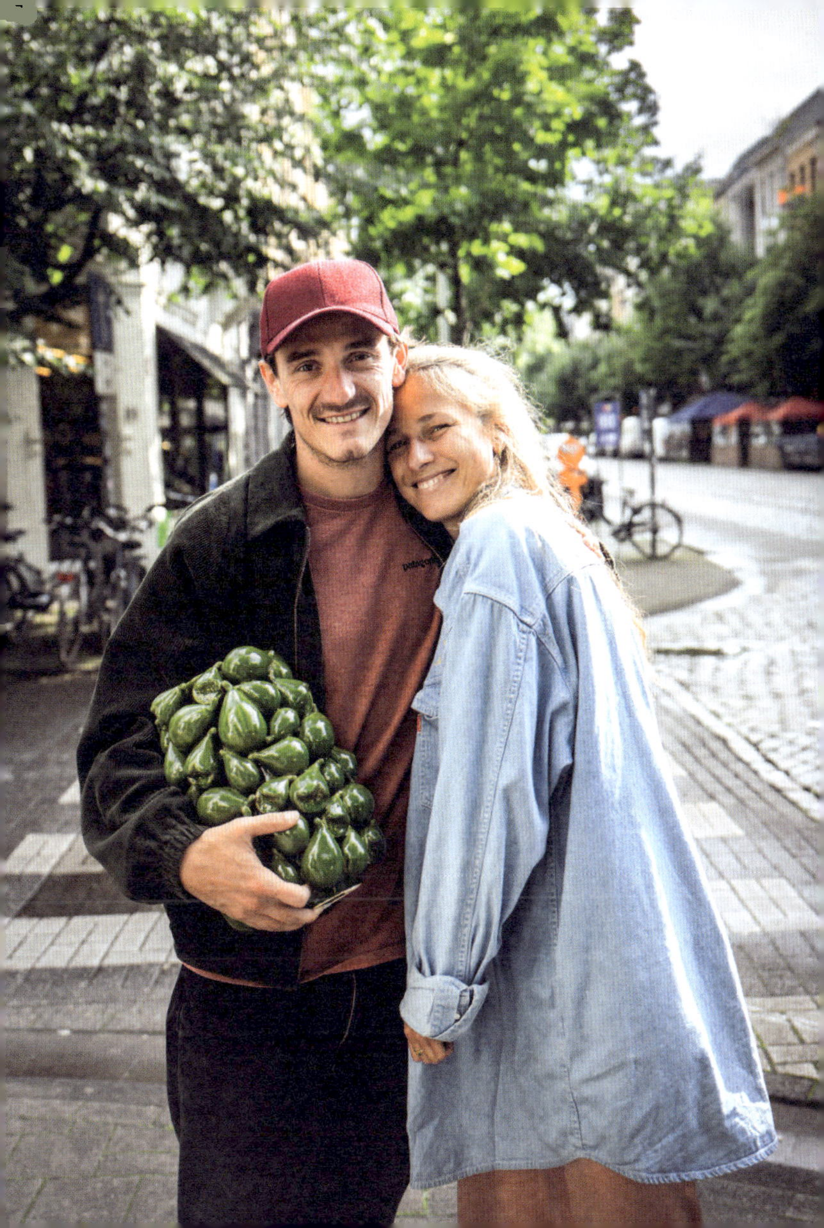

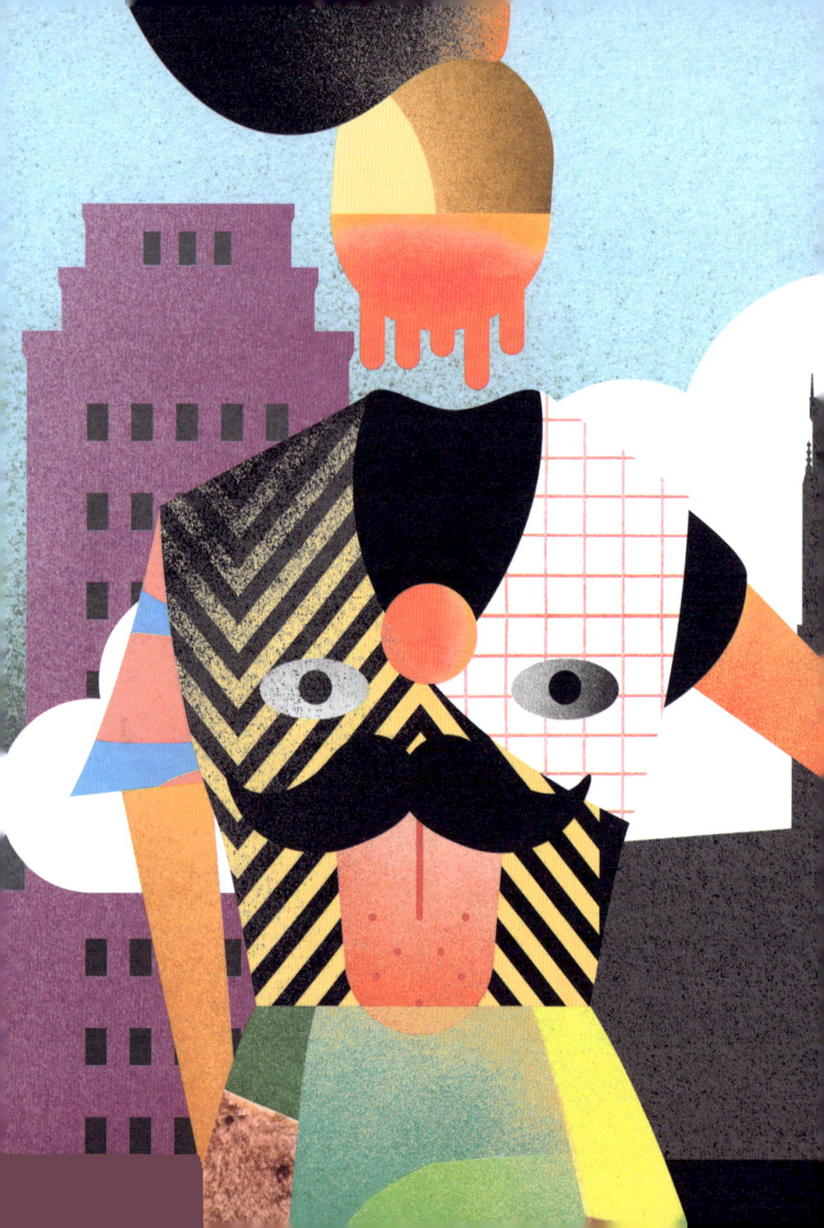

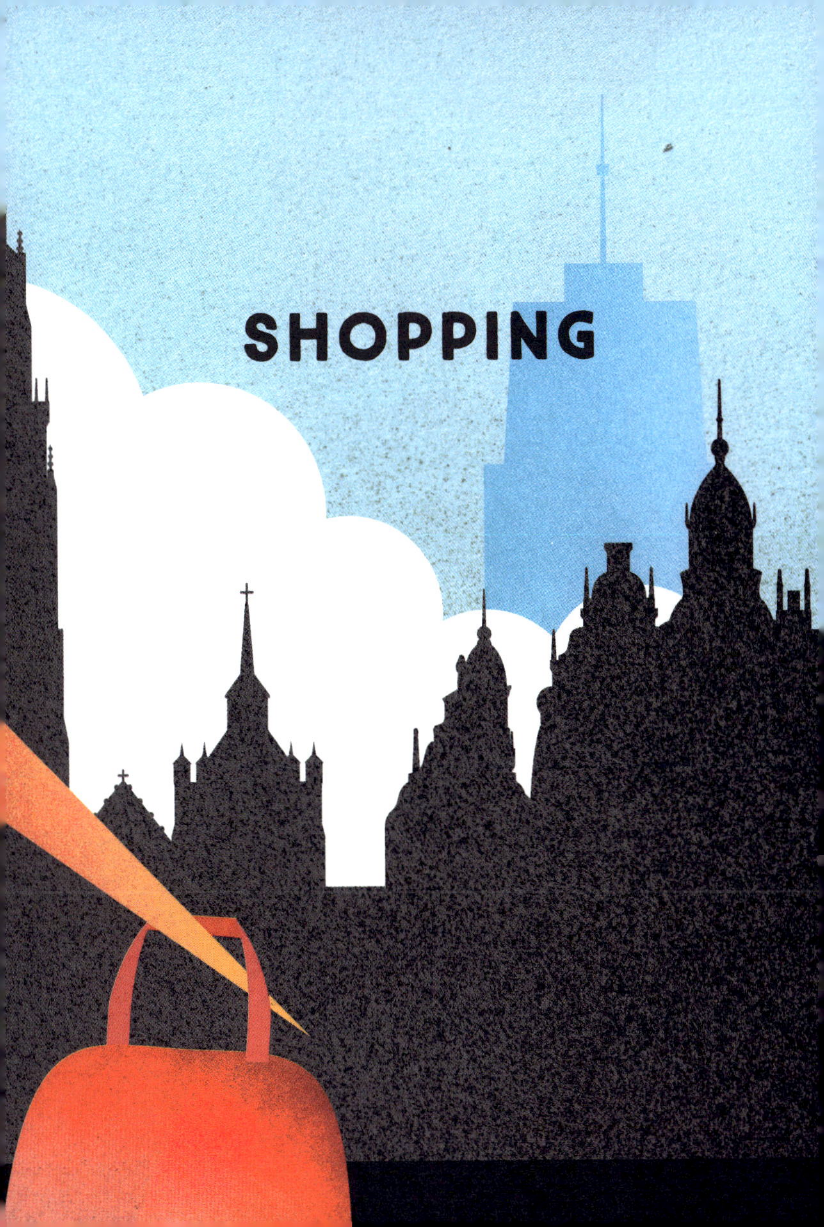
SHOPPING

# HOW TO DRESS LIKE A LOCAL

Dressing like an Antwerpenaar means embracing a style that is both effortlessly chic and eclectic, reflecting the city's fashion-forward reputation and its diverse cultural influences. Here are some tips to help you achieve that Antwerp look.

Start with a foundation of classic basics such as timeless trousers, a crisp T-shirt, and a well-fitted jumper or worker jacket. Invest in high-quality fabrics that not only look good but also are comfortable to wear. Add a twist by incorporating unexpected details, like bold patterns or uncommon textures, to showcase your individuality.

Elevate your look with statement accessories that add personality and flair, like chunky jewellery, colourful scarves, or standout footwear to inject a pop of style into your outfit. Don't be afraid to mix and match accessories to create a look that's uniquely yours.

Antwerp's unpredictable weather calls for stylish layering. Experiment by combining different garments, such as lightweight jumpers over collared shirts, or oversized coats paired with wide-leg trousers. Mixing and matching textures and colours adds depth to your ensemble while keeping you prepared for any weather changes. And don't forget your matching knitted beanie!

But above all, wear your outfit with confidence and grace. The key to dressing like an Antwerp local is not to follow fashion trends, but about expressing your own sense of style with confidence and self-assurance. Own your look, and you'll effortlessly blend in with the fashionable crowd of Antwerp.

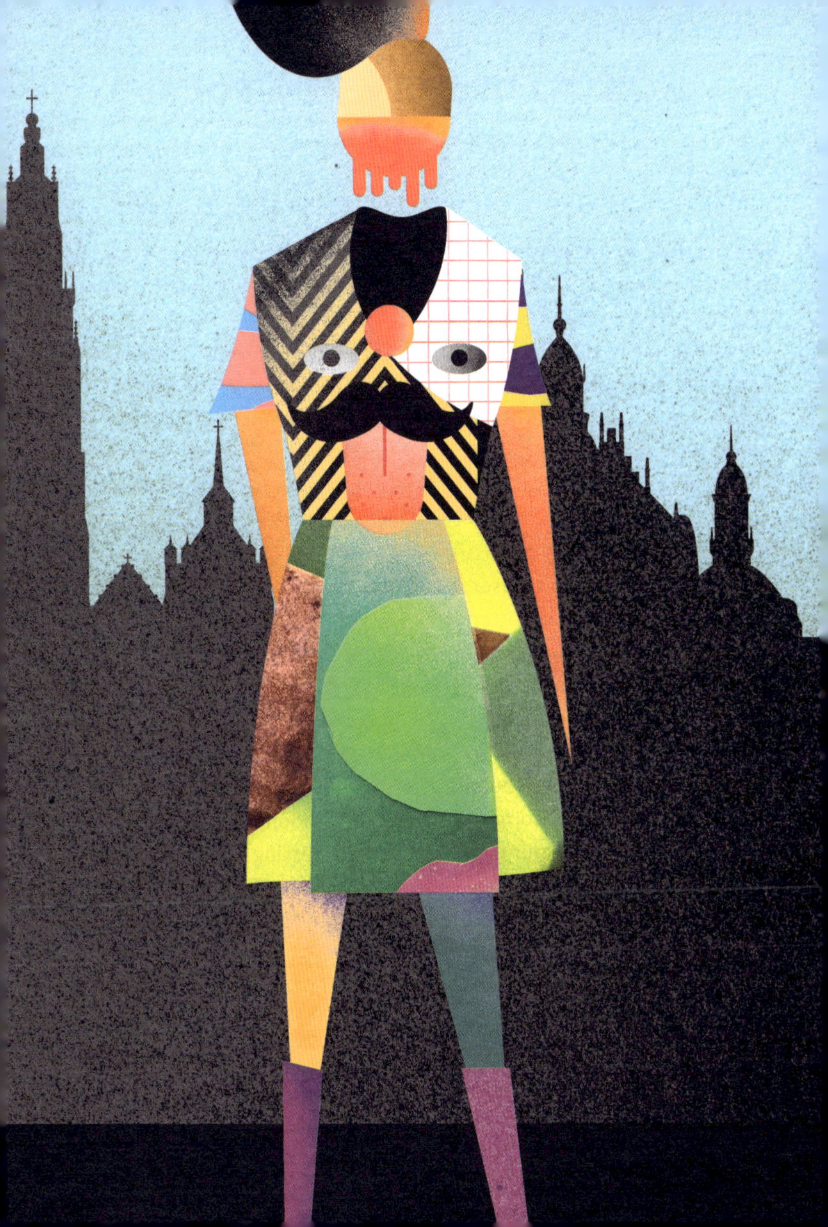

# FLEA MARKETS, VINTAGE & SECOND-HAND

**Think Twice**

*thinktwice-secondhand.be*

This isn't just a shop: Think Twice is an organisation with five Antwerp locations that gives back to the community through human/sustainable development projects and environment protection projects. Step inside any of its settings, and you will find items ranging from bohemian chic to retro glam and fashionable basics. They work in a five-week cycle, so there is always something new to discover.

**Brocantwerpen**

*Grote Markt, Centrum, brocantwerp.be*

This market is a true treasure trove of antiquities in the heart of Antwerp's Historical Centre. The stalls are filled with vintage finds, from antique furniture to collectible curiosities, clothing to jewellery, and books to vinyl. The market takes place about once a month from April to September.

**Dressing Circles**

*Blauwmoezelstraat 9, Centrum, dressingcircles.com*

Step into a world where vintage charm meets contemporary elegance. The curated selection at Dressing Circles contains quality pieces of colourful clothes and extraordinary accessories. From classic silhouettes to avant-garde designs, Dressing Circles invites you to elevate your style with a touch of vintage sophistication.

FLEA MARKETS, VINTAGE & SECOND-HAND 143

**Ensō Vintage**

*Lombardenvest 20,*
*Centrum, ensovintage.com*

At Ensō, they strive for a zero-waste future through a hand-picked selection of vintage, new upcycling collections, and designer pieces. Their designs are timeless and made from high-quality vintage items like clothes, tote bags, jewellery, leather goods and objects.

**Episode**

*Kammenstraat 14,*
*Centrum, episode.eu*

Episode is a European second-hand retail chain, and a sanctuary for the fashion-forward and nostalgic alike. Lose yourself in its eclectic mix of pre-loved garments, each with its own story to tell. Whether you're hunting for a statement piece or a timeless classic, you can find it here. Every item is checked, repaired if necessary, and washed before it hits the shelves.

**Jutka & Riska**

*Nationalestraat 87,*
*Centrum,*
*jutkaenriska.com*

Step into Jutka & Riska and immerse yourself in a world where bohemian flair meets vintage charm. From flowing fabrics to bold patterns, each piece exudes a sense of free-spirited individuality. They offer a lot of accessories such as vintage jewellery, sunglasses, belts, and bags, to complete your look.

**Kringwinkel**

*Lange Koepoortstraat*
*39, Historical Centre,*
*kringwinkel.be*

This community-driven initiative is dedicated to giving new life to pre-loved items. Browse through its eclectic array of clothes, furniture, and household goods, knowing that every purchase supports social and environmental causes. With each treasure you find, you're not just shopping – you're making a difference.

**Labels Inc.**

*Nationalestraat 95, Centrum, labelsinc.be*

Labels Inc. is a destination for fashion enthusiasts seeking vintage luxury and style. Explore its edited collection of pre-loved designer clothes, accessories, and rare finds. Each piece is meticulously selected for its quality and craftsmanship, and Belgian fashion labels and foreign luxury brands hang side by side.

**Melting Pot Kilo**

*Nationalestraat 14, Centrum, meltingpotkilo.com*

At Melting Pot Kilo, nostalgia comes by the pound as you sift through racks of vintage treasures. Embrace the thrill of the hunt as you scour through clothing, shoes, accessories, and bags, all priced by weight at €15 per kilo.

**Pardaf**

*Gemeentestraat 8, Centrum, pardaf.be*

Since 1973, three generations have immersed themselves in this family business in search of the best vintage designer fashion. They offer a wide range of clothes, jewellery, accessories, handbags, and shoes for children, men, and women.

**ROsier 41**

*Rosier 41, Centrum, rosier41.be*

At ROsier 41, you'll find high-fashion labels from Belgian designers like Dries Van Noten, Ann Demeulemeester, Maison Martin Margiela, and Raf Simons. Well-known foreign luxury brands are available too. From classic silhouettes to bold statement pieces, ROsier 41 invites you to embrace your individuality and express yourself through fashion.

**Riot Vintage Shop**

*Lange Koepoortstraat 46, Historical Centre, insta @riotsecondhand*

A haven for the fashion rebel, where vintage finds collide with contemporary edge. Explore its edgy selection of clothes and accessories, each piece infused with a sense of rebellion and individuality.

**De Slegte**

*Wapper 5, Centrum, deslegte.com*

A literary wonderland filled with countless second-hand books. Explore its shelves stocked with a diverse array of titles from timeless classics to obscure gems waiting to be found. The shelves are filled with almost every genre imaginable, from art and culture to travel and cooking, history and philosophy, and to fiction and autobiographies.

**Spul**

*Ommeganckstraat 85, Centrum, spul-antwerp.com*

An accumulation of curiosities and collectibles, with an eclectic array of vintage finds. At Spul, you'll find hoodies and jumpers, shirts, jackets, sports tops, hats, and beanies from the seventies to the nineties.

**Sunday Flea Market**

*Sint-Jansvliet, Centrum*

The Sunday Flea Market at Sint-Jansvliet is a vibrant celebration of Antwerp's eclectic spirit, where vendors gather to showcase their wares in a lively atmosphere. Browse through stalls brimming with paintings, antiques, books, tableware, and curiosities. Every Sunday from 9am to 5pm.

**Winckle**

*Lombardenstraat 6, Centrum, insta @winckle_winkel*

Rewind the clock and rediscover the allure of vintage fashion. Mother Chaja and daughter Ruby have carefully curated a selection of clothes and accessories. From timeless classics to one-of-a-kind treasures, Winckle invites you to embrace the past while crafting a style that is all your own.

**Boekenmarkt**

*De Coninckplein, North*

At Boekenmarkt De Conickplein you can find literary treasures in a sea of second-hand books and comics. Browse through stalls overflowing with vintage novels, rare editions, and forgotten classics every third Sunday of the month between 10am and 4pm.

**Oxfam Boutique**

*Brederodestraat 27, East/South, oxfambelgie.be*

Browse through the Boutique's carefully selected collection of pre-loved clothes, accessories, books, and home deco, knowing that every purchase supports Oxfam's mission to fight poverty and injustice around the world.

**Kringwinkel Circuit**

*Jef Cassiersstraat 29, South, kringwinkel.be*

Kringwinkel Circuit invites you to join the cycle of sustainability and style, where pre-loved treasures find new homes. You will find a unique selection of vintage items like clothes, small home decor items, and books at affordable prices.

# STREETWEAR

**Arte Antwerp**

*Kammenstraat 45, Centrum, arte-antwerp. com*

Known for its unique and artistic approach to streetwear, Arte offers clothes that blend urban style with creative designs. Expect bold graphics, vibrant and dark colours, and a distinct aesthetic that sets them apart in the streetwear scene.

**Castart + Our Sister**

*Lombardenvest 62, Centrum, castartclothing.com*

This brand combines the expertise of Castart, known for its urban clothing and accessories for men, with the flair of Our Sister, which focuses on women's streetwear. Together, they offer a diverse range of streetwear apparel, blending contemporary fashion with a street-smart edge. Nice to know: *Castart* is French for 'cheeky man'.

**Façon Jacmin**

*Kammenstraat 58, Centrum, faconjacmin.com*

Founded by Belgian twin sisters Alexandra and Ségolène, Façon Jacmin is an eco-conscious brand with an attitude. Specialising in high-quality denim garments, the brand emphasizes minimalist designs, impeccable craftsmanship, and sustainable production practices. Façon Jacmin's collections feature timeless pieces such as jeans, jackets, and skirts, crafted from premium fabrics and designed to endure the test of time.

**Lockwood Avenue**

*IJzerenwaag 3, Centrum, lockwood-avenue.com*

A fusion of skate culture and streetwear fashion, Lockwood Avenue brings together the best of both worlds. With a focus on quality craftsmanship and contemporary design, the brand offers a range of skate-inspired apparel and accessories that resonate with urban youth culture. Expect bold graphics, loose fits, and functional pieces that are perfect for the streets.

**Monar & Clothes**

*Everdijstraat 35, Centrum, monar.be*

Known for its premium brands, Monar offers elevated streetwear pieces that blend urban style with high-end fashion sensibilities. Their clothes, trainers, and accessories cater to those who appreciate refined urban attire.

**VIER**

*Theodoor van Rijswijckplaats 4, Centrum, vierantwerp.com*

VIER is a streetwear shop that encapsulates the essence of Antwerp's urban culture. With a focus on impactful designs, VIER offers a range of clothes, footwear, and accessories that reflect the city's diverse and dynamic street scene.

**Eat Dust**

*Volkstraat 2, South, eatdustclothing.com*

With a rugged and rebellious vibe, Eat Dust specialises in high-quality denim and workwear-inspired clothing. Their designs often feature vintage elements, sturdy finishes, and durable materials, appealing to those who appreciate an outspoken aesthetic and long-lasting garments. They also have a strong women's fashion line called Girls of Dust.

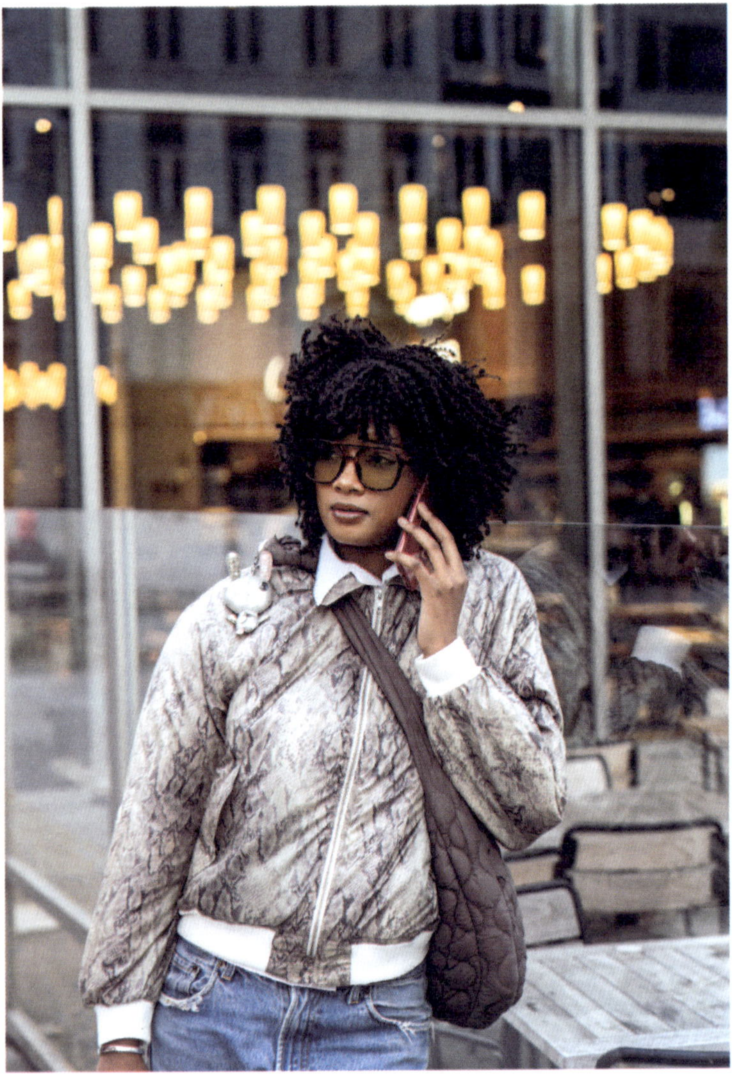

STREETWEAR

# ANTWERP FASHION

Antwerp retailers have two official sales periods (called *solden*), which start on 1st January and 1st July. The Antwerp Designer Sales also take place twice a year, in May and November. For one week, pop-up locations of genuine Antwerp Design at reduced prices appear in the city, consisting of older collections and sample sales. Keep an eye on *weekend.knack.be* for future dates and participating brands.

**Essentiel Antwerp**

*essentiel-antwerp.com*

Essentiel Antwerp is a vibrant and eclectic fashion brand known for its playful designs and bold colour palettes. Offering a wide range of clothing, accessories, and footwear, Essentiel Antwerp injects a sense of fun into contemporary fashion. From statement prints and eye-catching patterns to quirky embellishments and unexpected details, Essentiel Antwerp's collections exude a sense of joy and individuality. The brand has two shops and an outlet store in the city.

**Dries Van Noten**

*Nationalestraat 16, Centrum, driesvannoten.com*

Dries Van Noten is a renowned Belgian fashion designer known for his eclectic and artistic approach to clothing. His brand offers luxurious ready-to-wear collections characterised by rich fabrics, vibrant prints, and meticulous attention to detail. Dries Van Noten's designs often blend elements of classic tailoring with contemporary aesthetics, resulting in pieces that exude sophistication and individuality. Great for window shopping.

**Renaissance**

*Lange Gasthuisstraat 16, Centrum, princess.eu*

This multi-brand store offers a curated selection of high-end fashion brands. It showcases a diverse range of clothes, accessories, and lifestyle products, reflecting the latest trends and innovations in contemporary fashion. With its unique blend of luxury and streetwear aesthetics, Renaissance provides a platform for both established and up-and-coming talents in the fashion industry.

**Ann Demeulemeester**

*Leopold de Waelplaats, South, anndemeulemeester.com*

A prominent figure in the Belgian fashion scene, Ann Demeulemeester is celebrated for her avant-garde designs and poetic sensibility. Her brand showcases a distinct blend of romanticism and rebellion, with flowing silhouettes, intricate drapery, and a monochromatic colour palette. Ann Demeulemeester's designs often evoke a sense of mystery and drama, appealing to those who appreciate fashion as an expression of personal identity. Her pieces are expensive, but one can always dream.

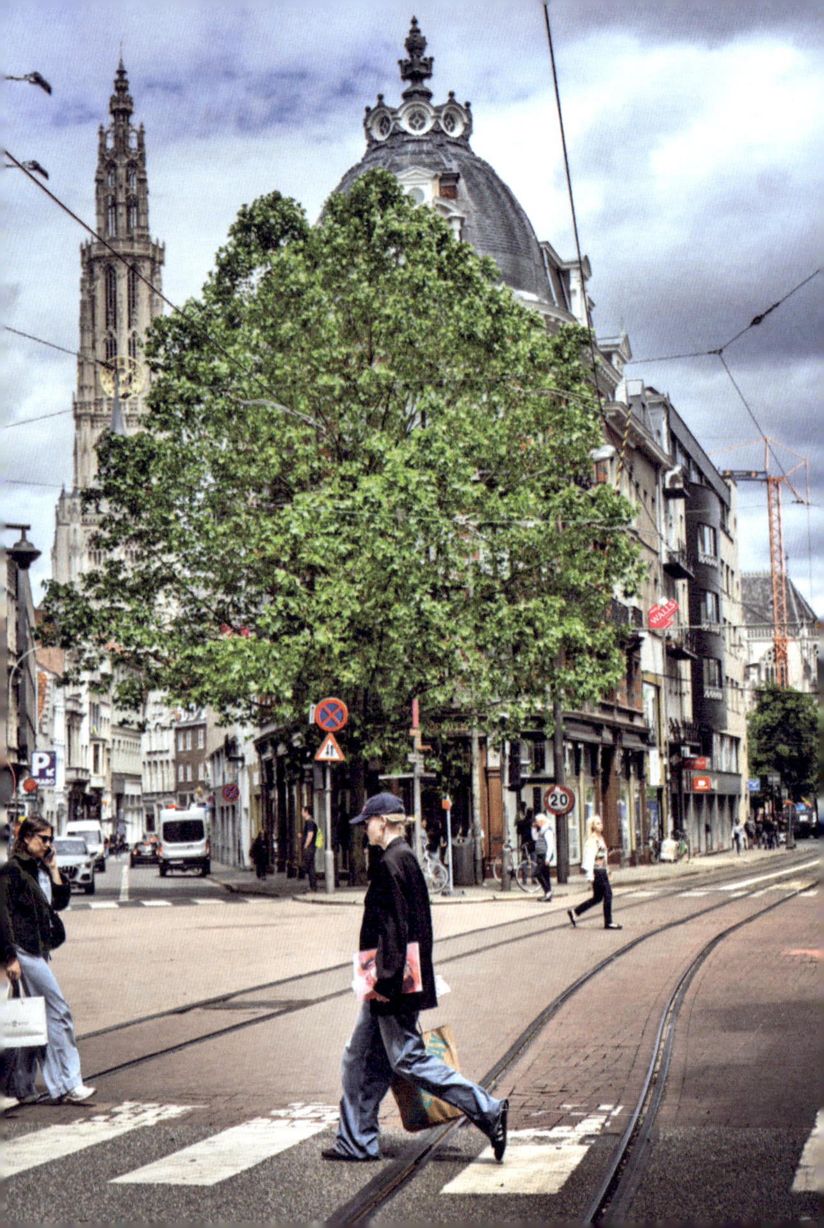
WALLS
20

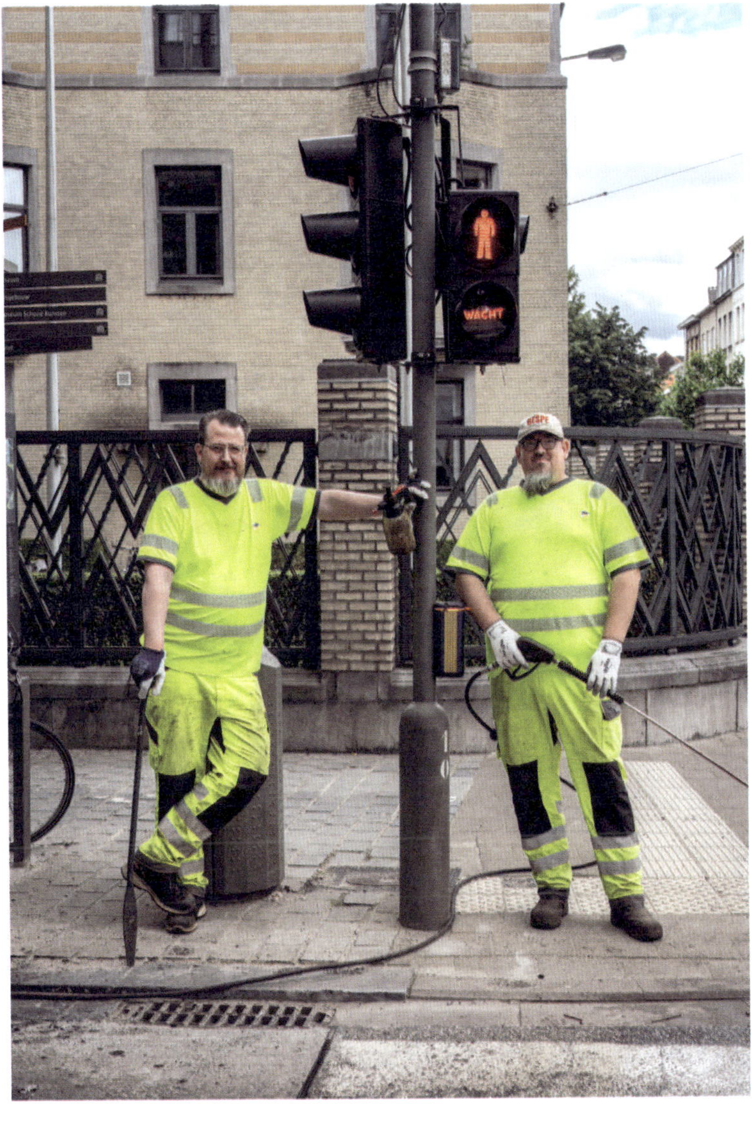
WACHT

# BOOKSHOPS

**BAI**

*Hoogstraat 62-64,
Centrum, baiantwerp.be*

BAI is a bookshop specialised in art books, architecture, and design. It offers a selection of publications on contemporary art, photography, fashion, and urbanism. This treasure trove for cultural and art goodies is also an ideal spot for finding gifts like notebooks, cards, and pens.

**Bookz&Booze**

*Gierstraat 2, Centrum,
bookznbooze.be*

According to Bookz&Booze, every special book pairs with a unique drink. Choose from their quirky selection of books, graphic novels, comics, and vinyl with their matching – often exclusive – drinks.

**Fnac**

*Meir 66, Centrum, fnac.be*

A large chain of bookstores, Fnac offers a wide selection of books, music, movies, electronics, and multimedia products. It caters to a diverse audience, with sections dedicated to fiction, non-fiction, comic books, and almost every theme imaginable.

**De Groene Waterman**

*Wolstraat 7, Centrum,
groenewaterman.be*

As a well-established independent bookshop, De Groene Waterman is known for its focus on quality literature and progressive values. It features a diverse selection of books on topics such as politics, social issues, philosophy, and fiction. They also host literary events, author readings, and discussions on current affairs, making it a hub for intellectual and cultural engagement.

**IMS International Magazine Store**

*Kaasrui 11, Centrum, imstijdschriften. beCentrum, baiantwerp.be*

Specialising in a wide range of magazines, IMS covers topics such as fashion, design, art, lifestyle, and current affairs. In addition to magazines, IMS also offers a selection of international newspapers, books, and stationery. It serves as a go-to destination for those seeking the latest publications from around the world.

↓ STAD LEEST

**Luddites Books & Wine**

*Hopland 34, Centrum,*
*luddites.be*

Luddites Books & Wine combines a love for literature with a selection of fine wines. Customers can browse through their collection of books while enjoying a glass of wine or coffee. The shop often hosts literary events and cocktail nights.

**The Other Shop**

*Melkmarkt 31, Centrum,*
*theothershop.be*

Quirky books, photography & coffee table books, and inspirational lifestyle books line the shelves at The Other Shop. It also is a gift shop with a selection of mugs, tote bags, postcards, stationery, puzzles, games, 3D craft, home deco, and much more.

**Stad Leest**

*Oudaan 18, Centrum,*
*stadleest.be*

This spacious and bright bookshop offers a diverse range of Dutch and English books for all ages and interests. It is also the place to find a quirky greeting card or some good tunes on vinyl. Their café offers lunch, coffee, and fresh pastries, including homemade scones.

**Standaard Boekhandel**

*Schoenmarkt*
*16-18, Centrum,*
*standaardboekhandel.be*

Get lost in the literary wonderland of Standaard Boekhandel, a large chain of bookshops offering a wide range of books and stationery. It caters to a broad audience with Dutch, English, and French books in all kinds of genres.

**Wunderkammer**

*Kleine Markt 14, Centrum,*
*wunderkammer.be*

Wunderkammer features a selection of books focusing on art, design, interior, and cooking inspiration. These books complement the shop's eclectic range of stationery (see page 161).

**Alta Via travel books**

*Nassaustraat 29, North, altaviatravelbooks.be*

Catering to travellers and adventure enthusiasts, Alta Via offers a selection of travel guides, maps, and books on hiking, backpacking, and exploration. Alta Via aims to inspire travellers for their next journey, whether it is a weekend getaway or an epic expedition.

**Cosimo**

*Scheldestraat 79, South, boekhandelcosimo.be*

Cosimo, formerly known as Buchbar, is a bookshop and publishing house with a pleasant and inviting ambiance. It offers a carefully considered selection of Dutch and English books across various genres. In the seating area you can relax or read your latest purchase while enjoying a cup of coffee or tea.

**CronopiO**

*Kasteelpleinstraat 21, South, cronopio.be*

This is the perfect neighbourhood bookshop. It has a café where locals meet for a cup of coffee or a glass of wine. Or enjoy their latest purchase. It has a good selection of Dutch and English fiction, non-fiction, poetry, and cookbooks. With its charming ambiance and welcoming atmosphere, it offers more than just books; it's a cultural hub where literature, art, and community converge.

**Erik Tonen Books**

*Kasteelpleinstraat 21, South, cronopio.be*

This shop specialises in rare editions, first editions, and collectible books, catering to collectors, scholars, and bibliophiles. Erik Tonen Books is known for its extensive collection of rare and antiquarian books, spanning various genres and subjects.

*Kloosterstraat 48, South, erik-tonen-books.com*

# ART SUPPLIES

**Academia**

*Mutsaardstraat 38,
Centrum, academia.be*

Academia is a family business with over ninety years of expertise. It is a go-to destination for art students and professionals seeking high-quality supplies. The shop specialises in professional-grade materials, including artist-quality paints, pencils, markers, paper, and premium brushes.

**De Banier**

*Kipdorp 30, Centrum,
debanier.be*

Known for its extensive range of art and craft supplies, De Banier caters to both professional artists and hobbyists. Go there for paint, drawing utensils, decoration supplies, clay, yarn, crafting kits, and instructions to explore new techniques or projects.

**Wunderkammer**

*Kleine Markt 14, Centrum,
wunderkammer.be*

Wunderkammer (see page 158 and pictures on the left) also stands out for its eclectic collection of art supplies and stationery, focusing on paper, pens, washi tape, notebooks, stickers, stamps, and fun office tools.

**De Wieuw**

*Scheldestraat 59, South,
dewieuw.be*

Renowned for its extensive array of art supplies, De Wieuw caters to a multitude of artistic requirements. From paints and brushes to canvas and drawing tools, De Wieuw offers a wide range of materials for both amateur and professional artists.

# AFFORDABLE ART AND HOME DECO

**Jacob's Conceptstore**

*Hoogstraat 73, Centrum, jacobsconceptstore.com*

Known for its carefully considered collection, Jacob's Conceptstore offers home deco, jewellery, and lifestyle items. They display works by artists who focus on one specific product. The result is a great mix of handmade and locally produced pieces that reflect current design trends.

**Uniek Gerief**

*Kleine Pieter Potstraat 19, Centrum, uniekgerief.be*

Uniek Gerief is a boutique specialising in retro home decor items and quirky curios. Discover a range of vintage ceramics, tableware, lamps, vases, and decorative objects that give your interior a personal and distinctive touch.

**Anna + Nina**

*Oever 6, South, anna-nina.nl*

This colourful boutique offers a unique blend of art, jewellery and home decor items, with a selection of products characterised by their bohemian, eclectic, and contemporary style. Browse through a range of decorative objects, textiles, candles, mugs, and accessories that add personality to your home.

**Kloosterstraat**

*Kloosterstraat, South*

Wander down this legendary street, lined with vintage and antique shops, as well as some boutiques offering new items. Step inside **Christiaensen & Christiaensen** for a selection of vintage furniture, home deco, and accessories with a focus on mid-century modern design. Dive into the Scandinavian-inspired and design-focused **Espoo** for furniture, tableware, lifestyle, and decorative objects. Don't miss the eclectic mix of home deco, skin care, sunglasses, and curiosities at **The Recollection**. And find affordable vintage paintings and drawings at **La Boîte Ouverte**.

↓ KLOOSTERSTRAAT

# RECORD SHOPS

**Backtrack**

*Sint-Katelijnevest 40,
Centrum,
fb @backtrackrecordshop*

Since 1996, Backtrack has offered a wide array of vinyl, CDs, DVDs, merchandise, and music-related books. Its selection spans various genres, including rock, pop, hip-hop, jazz, blues, and reggae. They offer both new releases and vintage classics.

**Bananarama**

*Pelikaanstraat 3/1280,
Centrum, insta@
bananaramavinyl*

Check out this musical wonderland with a wide choice of different genres. It's an abundance of new pressings and vintage LPs, singles, and CDs, all neatly stacked and organised in banana boxes.

**Grey**

*Korte Nieuwstraat 6,
Centrum, greyrecords.nl*

As they say themselves, Grey selects the most beautiful, weirdest, and original 33 and 45 RPM vinyl from all over the world. The owners' own record label, Grey Productions, brings the coolest underground sounds they can find, ranging from punk and Lo-fi, to garage and psychedelic, to surf with cold wave elements.

**The Record Collector**

*Kaasrui 4, Centrum,
therecordcollector.be*

This charming and independent second-hand record shop specialises in jazz, bossa nova, soul, blues, and classic pop & rock. It's a time-travel through music history, hopping between several decades and genres.

**Sugar Pie**

*Gierstraat 3, Centrum, fb
@sugarpierecords*

This is the latest addition to the city's record shops. Sugar Pie Records originated from owners Jan and Hans' personal collection, which has since been expanded with vintage vinyl and recent releases. They share a passion for eclecticism, so you can find almost anything here.

**Tune Up**

*Melkmarkt 20, Centrum, fb @tuneuprecords*

Find old and new quality vinyl at Tune Up, a shop that is also a meeting point for music lovers and musicians, hosting in-store performances. The collection ranges from hip-hop to new wave, pop to rock, and includes a very extensive choice of jazz.

**Wally's Groove World**

*Lange Nieuwstraat 126, Centrum, insta @ wallysgrooveworld*

Since 1997, owner Koen has amassed a vast collection of approximately 300,000 records, creating a vinyl universe of epic proportions. Explore this sprawling record emporium stocked with both fresh and pre-loved vinyl, singles, and cassettes. It specialises in house, techno, and various electronic genres.

**Warrecords**

*Sint-Katelijnevest 42, Centrum, warrecords.be*

This eclectic record shop offers more than just vinyl — they provide opportunities for aspiring artists through their 'Window Sessions', a platform for budding talent to shine. Besides selling records, they host events, workshops, listening sessions, and vinyl releases.

**Chelsea Records**

*Kloosterstraat 10, South, fb @chelsearecords*

At the oldest and largest record store in Belgium you will find an extensive collection of vinyl, around 60,000 CDs, 120,000 singles, picture discs and cassettes. Chelsea Records is also known for special editions and collectors' items.

↓ TUNE UP

# SHOPS WE LOVE

**A. Boon**

*Lombardenvest 2, Centrum, glovesboon.be*

This specialty shop from 1884 is known for its exclusive glove collection. The owners have maintained the Art Deco character of the shop, and the original glove boxes, counters, cabinets, and chairs turn Boon into an experience. They have over 10,000 pairs of gloves in stock, in all types of leather and in a range of colours.

**Mattheus B**

*Kleine Markt 8, Centrum, mattheusb.be*

Since 1907, Mattheus B has been a haven for tea and coffee lovers, offering an extensive selection of premium teas and coffees sourced from around the world. In this shop, you can also find accessories and equipment for brewing the perfect cup. Explore a variety of flavours, blends, and brewing methods, guided by the knowledgeable staff.

**Philip's Biscuits**

*Korte Gasthuisstraat 39, Centrum, philipsbiscuits.online*

This charming bakery is celebrated for its artisanal biscuits in the city known as *Koekenstad* ('Cookie City'). Try the famous Antwerp biscuit *Antwerpse Handjes*, a butter biscuit with almond flakes. Or the French *palmier*, the Belgian *kletskop*, and *kattentongen* (cat's tongues). Each is handcrafted with care using quality ingredients.

**Kupuku**

*Driekoningenstraat 33, East/South, kupuku.be*

Kupuku is a charming boutique that offers an assortment of fun Japanese items. It features Japanese nano blocks, adorable mugs, quirky little gifts, bento box accessories, and cute cat-themed objects.

**Pawlov**

*Kasteelpleinstraat 57, South, pawlov.be*

Do you want to pamper your pet? Then explore Pawlov's selection of fun dog and cat toys, stylish collars, and hip accessories for your furry friend.

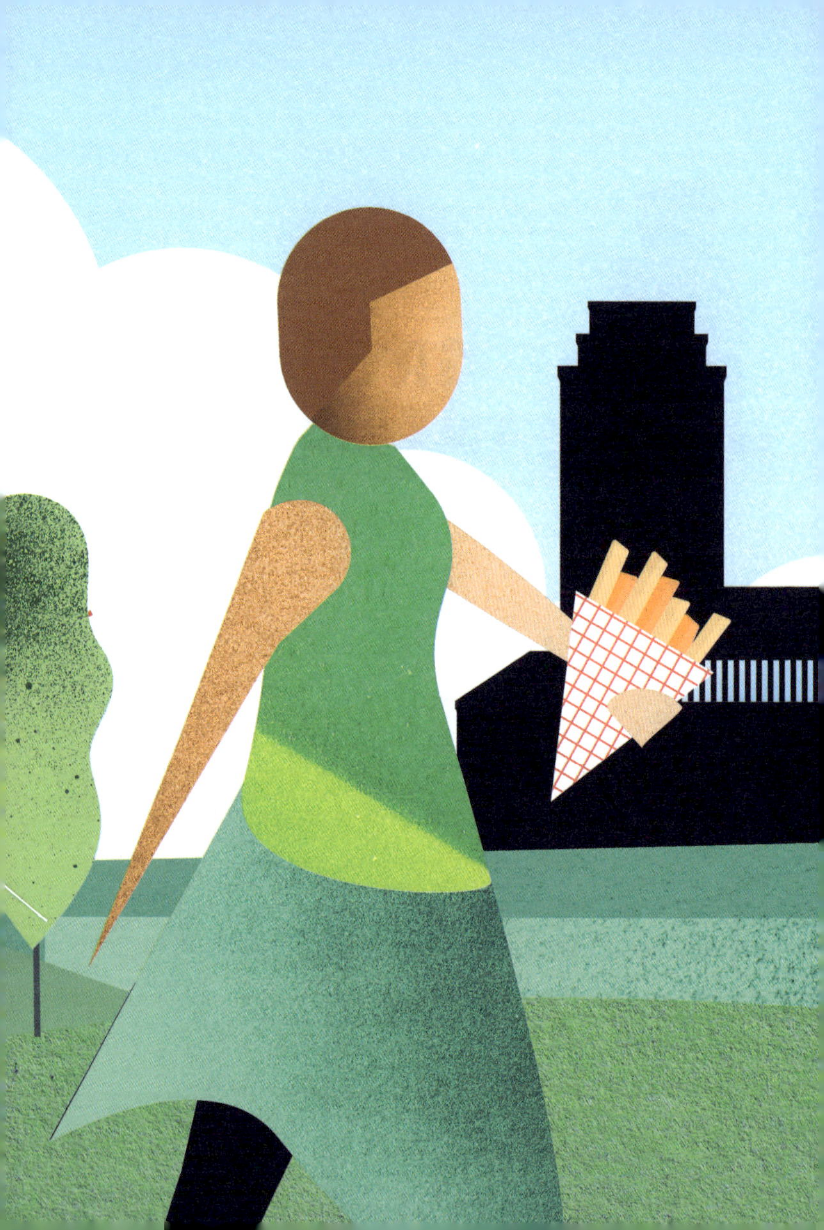

# GREEN ANTWERP

# PARKS & SWIMMING

### Botanische Tuin Den Botaniek

Created in the 16th century by pharmacist Peter van Coudenberghe, this botanic garden is small but stunning. He planted more than 600 different plants to prepare medicine for the adjacent St Elisabeth Hospital. It has a pond and a diverse collection of plants, trees, and flowers from around the world, including medicinal herbs and exotic species.
*Leopoldstraat 24, Centrum*

### Scheldekaaien

The quays along the Scheldt, called Scheldekaaien, offer scenic promenades and recreational spaces. The riverfront is popular for walking, jogging, and cycling, with panoramic views of the river, port, and skyline. On summer evenings, it's a popular spot for having a drink and some snacks while watching the sun set.
*Along the Scheldt River, Centrum & South*

### Stadspark

One of Antwerp's oldest and most iconic parks, Stadspark (City Park) is located near the city centre. It boasts expansive lawns, flower beds, and shaded pathways, providing a peaceful retreat from the hustle and bustle of urban life. In Stadspark, you'll also find statues, monuments, a historical bridge, and a duck pond.
*Between Rubenslei, Quinten Matsijslei & Van Eycklei, Centrum*

### Park Spoor Noord

This large urban park is located in the northern part of Antwerp. The former railway yard has been transformed into a modern green space with playgrounds, sports facilities (including table tennis tables, a *pétanque* court, basketball court, and a cricket cage), jogging paths, and picnic areas. Skaters and BMXers have

PARKS & SWIMMING

access to a skate bowl with a full pipe. The park often hosts events, festivals, and cultural activities, and during the summer months a lively bar is installed underneath the hangar.
*Between Ellermanstraat, Den Dam and Schijnpoort, North*

### Droogdokkenpark

This waterfront park is located near the old dry docks in Eilandje. It offers scenic views of the Scheldt River and the historic port area. The park features walking paths, green spaces, and benches to enjoy the maritime atmosphere and observe the city's industrial heritage.
*Droogdokkenweg, North*

### Boekenberg Swimming Pond

Boekenberg is a natural swimming pool located in the Deurne district of Antwerp. It features filtered and purified water without the use of chemicals, creating a refreshing and eco-friendly swimming experience. It also offers green areas for sunbathing and picnics. It is only open in summer.
*Van Baurscheitlaan 88, East*

### Groen Kwartier

This modern and car-free residential area is situated in a former military hospital complex. It has landscaped gardens and green spaces for residents and visitors to enjoy. Groen Kwartier ('Green Quarter') provides a tranquil oasis within the city, blending contemporary architecture with lush greenery. Attached to it is the creative PAKT area, which is a perfect place for coffee, lunch, dinner or drinks.
*Between Lange Leemstraat, Lamorinierestraat & Boomgaardstraat, East*

### Harmoniepark & Koning Albertpark

Located in the Harmonie neighbourhood, you will find these small but charming green spaces. Both parks offer opportunities for relaxation,

↓ PARK SPOOR NOORD

↓ ZUIDPARK

PARKS & SWIMMING

175

picnics, and outdoor recreation. You have to cross the road to get from one park to the other.
*Mechelsesteenweg, East*

**Zuidpark**

A picturesque stretched-out park in Het Zuid, where likely one of the biggest transformations of the city took place. At the end of the 19th century, three docks were dug at this location as an extension of the former port. But over the course of the 20th century, the port's activities moved mainly to Noord. In 1969, the Zuiderdokken were closed, and a parking lot for thousands of cars was created. Nowadays, it features lush green lawns, tree-lined pathways, and ornamental gardens. Here you can enjoy leisurely strolls, have a picnic and relax.
*Between Vlaamse Kaai & Waalse Kaai, South*

**Strand van Sint-Anneke**

Sint-Anneke Beach is a recreational area along the Scheldt River, offering sandy beaches, green lawns, and panoramic views of Antwerp's skyline. It is a popular destination for sunbathing and picnicking during the summer months. Even though it can be very tempting, swimming in the Scheldt River is not allowed. It's very dangerous due to shipping, tides, and strong currents.
*Wandeldijk, Linkeroever*

↓ STRAND VAN SINT-ANNEKE

# VEGETARIAN AND VEGAN

**Camion**

This vegan restaurant is renowned for its plant-based all-day breakfast and lunch options. Their menu is full of home-made goodies crafted from the freshest, organic, local, and seasonal ingredients. This approach is continued into their drinks, from their coffee to homemade lemonades, and natural wines. Whether you're craving a crunchy salad, a comforting soup, or their legendary signature toast *Camion Gekapt*, Camion has you covered.
*Paleisstraat 7, East/South, camion-ette.be*

**Falafel Tof**

Indulge in wallet-friendly and lip-smacking Middle Eastern delights, starring the unbeatable falafel. Take your pick between a bowl or pita and customise your meal with fresh veggies from the salad bar. Complete your meal with combo deals that include potato wedges and a drink.
*Hoogstraat 32, Centrum, fb @falafeltof*

**HART**

The seasons dictate the menu at HART, a plant-based brunch and dinner restaurant with tapas and pizza evenings. The owner's roots lie in Spain, Chile, and China, and this is reflected in the menu. From Spanish vegan tortillas and scrambled tofu to a Chilean hotdog. But homemade granola, vegan croissants and hearty sourdough sandwiches with healthy spreads also appear on the table.
*Minderbroedersrui 34, Centrum, hart-antwerpen.be*

↓ HUMM

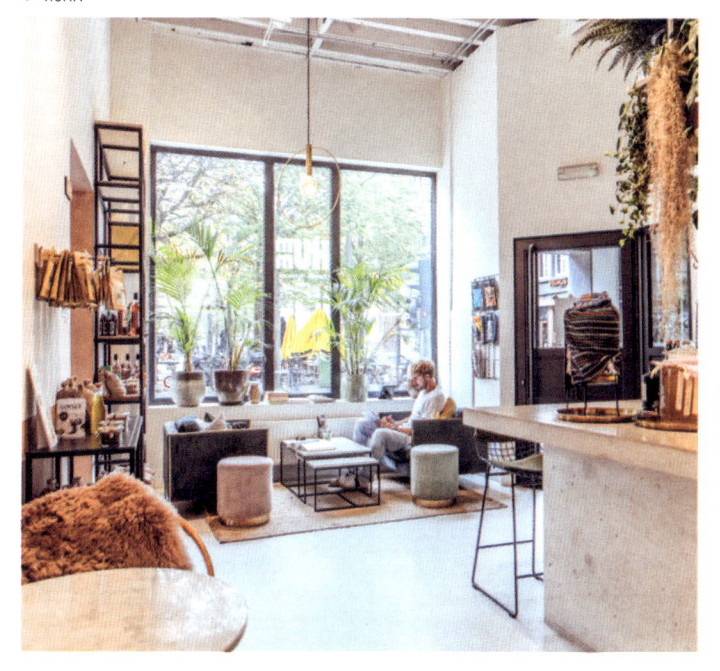

**Have a Roll**

Indulge in the daily delight of freshly baked cinnamon rolls at Have a Roll. Take your pick from a line-up of nine tantalising options, featuring seven beloved classics (like apple, nut, caramel pecan, and *speculaas (Biscoff)*) and two exciting monthly flavours. Plus, rejoice in the fact that all rolls are fully vegan, crafted without any dairy or eggs. As the icing on the cake (or rather, the roll), they're topped with a delicious plant-based cream cheese frosting.

*Oudaan 15/31, Centrum, havearoll.com*

### IceLab NiceCream

This vegan ice cream parlour is known for its delicious and creamy plant-based frozen desserts. It serves a variety of twelve vegan ice cream flavours, as well as waffles and pastries made with natural and pure ingredients. Flavours range from salty peanut and tiramisu, to *stroopwafels* and *speculaas* (Biscoff), to coffee and cheesecake, and several fruity options.
*Oudevaartplaats 38, Centrum, icelab.be*

### Lento

Lento is a highly regarded restaurant that has won multiple awards for being the best vegan restaurant in Belgium. It offers a diverse menu featuring creative and artfully presented plant-based dishes. The owners make it their mission to demonstrate that a plant-based menu can also be a very Burgundian experience.
*Oude Koornmarkt 44a, Centrum, restaurantlento.be*

### Humm

Middle Eastern vegetarian street food is the main character at Humm. It focuses on serving wholesome and nourishing food made from high-quality ingredients. Their menu boasts a delightful array of options, from all-day breakfast treats to shareable mezze dishes. Or you can choose from solo plates like hummus bowls, pitas loaded with eggplant and falafel, or wraps with seitan and mushrooms.
*Dageraadplaats 33, East, humm.love*

### Tastebuds

At Tastebuds, they believe that plant-based and sustainable food shouldn't be boring, and that it doesn't even have to be healthy either. That's why they like to call it Fun Food. Their varied menu with (loaded) fries, burgers, snacks (like cauli wings, mushroom croquettes and falafel waffles) is made without

any meat or fish. Everything is prepped with quality ingredients from small, local suppliers.
*Dageraadplaats 15, East, tastebudsantwerp.be*

### De Broers van Julienne

Whether it's lunch, afternoon tea, *apéro*, or dinner, they've got you covered at the oldest vegetarian restaurant of Antwerp. Their menu boasts an array of soul-warming soups, fresh salads, quiches, flatbreads, and exotic oven-baked dishes. In summer, you can dine in their enclosed garden, where the ambiance transports you to a Southern European town.
*Kasteelpleinstraat 45-47, South, debroersvanjulienne.be*

### CIRCUS

Delicious organic cuisine inspired by the supply of the field and local passionate producers. CIRCUS offers a menu featuring a mix of vegetarian, vegan, and gluten-free options. Try the Thai fusion salad, pulled oyster mushroom bun, or lentil burger with halloumi. If you have a sweet tooth, you will love their homemade pastries; vegan, free from refined sugars, and gluten-free. CIRCUS has several cosy corners and a hidden terrace at the back with space to sit alone, as a couple, or in larger groups.
*Kasteelpleinstraat 26, South, circusrestaurant.be*

# NON-FOOD

### Juttu

Juttu is a two-story lifestyle concept store that offers a diverse range of clothes, accessories, footwear, home goods, and beauty products from over a hundred sustainable and socially responsible brands. With ReJUsed, a selection of quirky vintage fashion & upcycled pieces is offered in a shop-in-shop that will make many vintage lovers' hearts beat faster.

*Meir 19, Centrum, juttu.be*

**BorGerHub**

Check out this vibrant eco-haven, which is stocked with locally made planet-loving products and ethical goods. It features a range of sustainable lifestyle items, including clothes, accessories, home goods, and personal care products. Complete your visit with a coffee at Plantbar Jacqueline, their lush plants and coffee shop.

*Turnhoutsebaan 92, East, insta @borgerhub*

**HOST**

At HOST, sustainability takes centre stage in their line-up of fashion and lifestyle offerings. Browse through their thoughtfully chosen range of clothes, accessories, skincare, and gifts; all crafted from eco-friendly materials and produced with ethical practices in mind. You are also welcome in their inviting bar for a coffee and something sweet.

*Statiestraat 56, East, host-concept.com*

**Supergoods**

Supergoods is your go-to destination for sustainable and ethically produced fashion and lifestyle items. Devoted to eco-consciousness, they offer a selection of guilt-free clothes, accessories, footwear, and cosmetics made from eco-friendly materials such as organic cotton, recycled fibres and natural dyes.

*Kloosterstraat 38, South, supergoods.be*

↓ CIRCUS

VEGETARIAN AND VEGAN

# OUTSIDE OF ANTWERP

**Axel Vervoordt Gallery**

*axel-vervoordt.com*

Back in 1857, this spot was all about brewing and distilling. These days it's shaking things up as an art gallery spread over a number of buildings. The gallery is known for its minimalist design and serene atmosphere, reflecting the aesthetic vision of Axel Vervoordt, a prominent Belgian art dealer and interior designer. It transcends traditional boundaries, offering visitors a multi-sensory journey through contemporary art and design, featuring works by renowned artists like Anish Kapoor, James Turrell, and Marina Abramovic. It is located in Wijnegem, about thirty minutes by car from Antwerp.

**Brussels**

*visit.brussels*

Belgium's bustling capital is steeped in centuries of history. This vibrant city has world-class museums and one of the prettiest squares in Europe, the Grand Place. Brussels is called the Capital of Europe, as the European Parliament and European Commission are located here. With its cultural diversity, it is a melting pot with influences from across the world, making it a dynamic and cosmopolitan destination. From Antwerpen-Centraal it takes about 45 minutes by train.

**Doel**

*koesterdoel.be*

Just a stone's throw from the Port of Antwerp lies 'ghost town' Doel. It is known for its many abandoned buildings and graffiti-covered houses. Due to its eerie atmosphere, it has become a popular spot for urban exploration and photography. Freely accessible on weekdays between 6am and 6pm. Getting there takes about thirty minutes by car.

**Fortengordel**

*fortengordels.be*

Antwerp's Fort Belt, also known as the Brialmont Fortifications, forms a ring of several late 19th century defensive structures surrounding the city. These forts were equipped with the latest military technology of the time to defend Antwerp from potential invasions. Each fort has its own history and unique architectural characteristics. The forts are located in various suburbs surrounding Antwerp, accessible by public transport or car.

**Mechelen**

*visit.mechelen.be*

With its rich history and stunning architecture, Mechelen offers a lot of old-world charm. Wander through the cobbled streets of its Historic Centre, and marvel at the beauty of the UNESCO listed St. Rumbold's Cathedral. Explore the Grote Markt (Market Square) with its centuries-old guild houses and impressive Town Hall. And don't miss the chance to visit the Palace of Margaret of Austria, a magnificent Renaissance palace that once served as the residence of the Habsburg regent. Complete your visit with a walk alongside the river over the floating part of the Dyle Towpath. About fifteen minutes by train from Antwerpen-Centraal.

**Nachtegalenpark**

*middelheimmuseum.be*

The Nachtegalenpark is the ideal spot if you want to spend some time in nature just outside of Antwerp. It consists of three parks: Vogelzang, Den Brandt, and Middelheim, and spans 80 hectares. **Middelheim** is a free open-air sculpture park known for its extensive collection of modern and contemporary art set in beautiful gardens. It even contains a statue of Auguste Rodin, one of the greatest sculptors of all time. **Den Brandt** has a charming castle, a small English cottage, and a reproduction of Michelangelo's David. The statue was purchased at the 1910 World Exhibition in Brussels. All three parks are easy to reach by bus or the Velo bicycle sharing service.

**Verbeke Foundation**

*verbekefoundation.com*

The Verbeke Foundation is not your typical art museum. It offers a surreal immersive experience, with art and nature coming together in unexpected ways. From larger-than-life sculptures to thought-provoking installations, every corner of the park is bursting with creativity. Wander through lush greenery, explore abandoned shipping containers-turned-art galleries, and encounter bizarre and beautiful works of art that challenge perceptions and ignite the imagination. Located in Kemzeke, approximately half an hour's drive from Antwerp but not accessible by public transport.

↓ NACHTEGALENPARK

↓ MIDDELHEIM

↓ AXEL VERVOORDT GALLERY

OUTSIDE OF ANTWERP

# INDEX

Districts 8
Travel 14
Where to stay 18
Good to know 23
When to travel 26
History 38
Sightseeing 46
Museums 54
Street art 62
Cinema 66
Festivals 70
Tours 72
Things to do 74
Famous people 78
Films & series in and about Antwerp 84
Books in & about Antwerp 88
Fun facts 92
Photo spots 96
Food & drinks 102
Going out 126
Shopping 138
Green Antwerp 170
Parks & swimming 172
Vegetarian and vegan 178
Outside of Antwerp 184

## AFFORDABLE ART AND HOME DECO 162
Anna + Nina 162
Jacob's Conceptstore 162
Kloosterstraat 162
Uniek Gerief 162

## ANTWERP FASHION 152
Ann Demeulemeester 153
Antwerp Six, The 80
Dries Van Noten 152
Essentiel Antwerp 152
Renaissance 153

## ART SUPPLIES 161

## BOOKSHOPS 156
Alta Via travel books 159
BAI 156
Bookz&Bookze 156
Cosimo 159
CronopiO 159
Erik Tonen Books 159
Fnac 156
Groene Waterman, De 156
IMS International Magazine Store 157
Luddites Books & Wine 158
Other Shop, The 158
Stad Leest 158
Standaard Boekhandel 158
Wunderkammer 158, 161

## FLEA MARKETS, VINTAGE & SECOND-HAND 142
Boekenmarkt 147
Brocantwerpen 142
Dressing Circles 142
Enso Vintage 144
Episode 144
Jutka & Riska 144
Kringwinkel 144
Kringwinkel Circuit 147
Labels Inc. 145
Melting Pot Kilo 145
Oxfam Boutique 147
Pardaf 145
Riot Vintage Shop 146
ROsier 41 145
Slegte, De 146
Spul 146
Sunday Flea Market 146
Think Twice 142
Winckle 147

## FOOD AND DRINKS 102
Aldo, Bakkerij, 106
Alma Libre 117

Andy Roasters 106
**Bakeries 106**
Balls & Glory 117
Barnini 110
Bia Mara 117
Black and Yellow 104
Boker Tov 115
**Breakfast & lunch 107**
**Bring the parents 122**
Butchers Coffee 106
Cafématic 111
Caffenation 104
Caffe Mundi 104
Camino 117
Charlie's Antwerpen 110
CHIPS 114
**Coffee & tea 104**
Dabba King 121
Dansing Chocola 121
**Dinner 115**
DOJO 2.0 122
Exotische Markt 111
Fiera 122
Finjan 122
**Frieten 114**
Frites Atelier 114
FUNK, Bakkerij 107
Goossens, Bakkerij 107
In de Roscam 119
Jean sur Mer 119
Kaffeenini 111
Kapitein Zeppos 119
Knees to Chin 119
KŪkai 105
Little Bún 115
Madonna Restaurant 123
Mission Masala 121
Nordica 31 112
Normo 104
Oats Day Long 107
Orso 121
Pici 115
Plump 120
Racine PAKT 114
Rush Rush 105

Quite Frankly 112
Satay 120
Sumac 122
Takumi 115
Tinsel 112
Vers Zuid 114
Via Via 121
Vogelenmarkt 111
Walvis 112

**GOING OUT 126**
Amber Bottle Shop 132
**Bars 128**
Beestenbos 128
Belgian Wines 132
Café Baron 130
Café Vitrin 130
Cargo Club 133
**Clubs 133**
Club Capital 133
Club Vaag 134
**Cocktails 132**
Den Draak 131
Dogma 132
Hessenhuis 131
IKON Antwerpen 134
In Den Boer van Tienen 129
Jones & Co 132
Kasko 133
Korsakov 128
Murkukutum 133
Muze, De 128
Patine 131
Plein Publiek 134
**Queer 131**
Revista 131
Titulus 133
Tram 3 129
**Wine 132**

**MUSEUMS 54**
Antwerp Story, The 54
Chocolate Nation 54
DIVA 54
FOMU Fotomuseum 58

KMSKA 60
M HKA 60
MAS 57
Mayer van den Bergh, Museum 56
MoMu 55
Plantin-Moretus, Museum 56
Rubenshuis 56
Red Star Line Museum 58

## PHOTO SPOTS 96
Centraal Station 96
Chinatown 96
Cranes, Old 100
Felix Pakhuis 99
Handelsbeurs 96
Havenhuis 99
MAS Rooftop Panorama 99
PAKT 100
Parkbrug 100
Vlaeykensgang 99

## RECORD SHOPS 164

## SHOPPING 138
How to dress like a local 140

## SHOPS WE LOVE 168

## SIGHTSEEING 46
Antwerpen-Centraal 46
Bootje, Het 52
Bourlaschouwburg 46
Brabofontein 46
Cogels-Osylei 52
Grote Markt 47
Havenhuis 52
Oldest house of Antwerp 50
Onze-Lieve-Vrouwekathedraal 50
Paleis op de Meir 50
Sint-Annatunnel 53
Sint-Carolus Borromeuskerk 51

Stadsfeestzaal 51
Vlaeykensgang 51
Voetgangerstunnel 53

## STREETWEAR 148
Arte Antwerp 148
Castart + Our Sister 148
Eat Dust 149
Façon Jacmin 148
Lockwood Avenue 149
Monar & Clothes 149
VIER 149

## VEGETARIAND AND VEGAN
BorGerHub 182
Broers van Julienne, De 181
Camion 178
CIRCUS 181
Falafel Tof 178
HART 178
Have A Roll 179
HOST 182
Humm 180
IceLab NiceCream 180
Juttu 181
Lento 180
Supergoods 182
Tastebuds 180

## WHERE TO STAY 18
A-STAY 18
Antwerp Central Hostel 18
Antwerp City Hostel 19
Ash Hotel, The 19
B&B Hotels 18
City Camping at Linkeroever 21
Citybox 19
Prizeotel 20
Yays 20
Yust 21

# ABOUT THE AUTHOR

**Lonneke Snel**

Lonneke Snel is a seasoned food and travel blogger who has called Antwerp home for the past decade. With a keen eye for the city's hidden treasures and new places to explore, her recommendations are a goldmine for young adults eager to experience the city like a local. From the best spots to grab a coffee and savour local cuisine to the must-see museums and exciting activities, these tips will make your visit to Antwerp unforgettable.

**WHY SHOULD I GO TO ANTWERP**
the city you definitely need to
visit before you turn 30

Published in 2024 by mo'media
P.O. Box 359, 3000 AJ Rotterdam,
The Netherlands, momedia.nl

**Concept**
mo'media

**Text and address selection**
Lonneke Snel

**Art direction and illustration design**
Jelle F. Post

**Editing**
Ezra van Wilgenburg

**Photography**
Vincent van den Hoogen, Marie Monsieur, Lonneke Snel, Dani van Oeffelen, Ezra van Wilgenburg, and others

**Special thanks to**
Youri Nieuwenhuijsen, and
Maaike van Steekelenburg

All rights reserved. No part of this publication may be copied, displayed, extracted, reproduced, utilised, stored in a retrieval system or transmitted in any form or by any means, electronic, mechanical or otherwise including but not limited to photocopying, recording, or scanning without the prior written permission of the publisher.

(m) Copyright © mo'media BV, 2024

Why Should I Go To Antwerp
ISBN 978 94 9333 844 9
NUR 510

**Disclaimer**
The points of interested mentioned in this travel guide have been selected by the author. None of them have been paid for inclusion in this book: the *Why Should I Go To* book series is entirely ad-free.

**Publisher's Note**
Every effort has been made to ensure that the information in this book is accurate at the time of going to press. The publisher welcomes any information or suggestions for correction or improvement. Please send us an e-mail at info@momedia.nl or a DM on Instagram.

📷 🎵 whyshouldigoto

---

**WHY SHOULD I GO TO?**
Information on all our travel guides on **WHYSHOULDIGOTO.COM**

**Why Should I Go To travel guides are available for the following cities**: Amsterdam, Antwerp, Barcelona, Berlin, Copenhagen, London, Paris, and Prague. More cities will be added soon. Check our socials for updates.